CHINESE CULTURE

CHARACTERS

HAN JIANTANG

 China Intercontinental Press

图书在版编目（CIP）数据

汉字：英文 / 韩鉴堂著；王国振，周玲译 . -- 北京 : 五洲传播出版社，2014.1（中国文化系列 / 王岳川主编）
ISBN 978-7-5085-2714-7

Ⅰ . ①汉… Ⅱ . ①韩… ②王… ③周… Ⅲ . ①汉字 — 文化 — 中国 — 英文 Ⅳ . ① H12

中国版本图书馆 CIP 数据核字 (2013) 第 321785 号

中国文化系列丛书

主　　编 : 王岳川
出 版 人 : 荆孝敏
统　　筹 : 付 平

中国文化·汉字

著　　者 : 韩鉴堂
翻　　译 : 王国政 周 玲
责 任 编 辑 : 苏 谦
插 图 绘 制 : 韩鉴堂 韩 宇
图 片 提 供 : CFP　FOTOE　东方 IC
装 帧 设 计 : 丰饶文化传播有限责任公司
出 版 发 行 : 五洲传播出版社
地　　址 : 北京市海淀区北三环中路 31 号生产力大楼 B 座 7 层
邮　　编 : 100088
电　　话 : 010-82005927，82007837
网　　址 : www.cicc.org.cn
承 印 者 : 北京利丰雅高长城印刷有限公司
版　　次 : 2014 年 1 月第 1 版第 1 次印刷
开　　本 : 889×1194mm 1/16
印　　张 : 14.5
字　　数 : 200 千字
定　　价 : 128.00 元

Contents

Preface

The Chinese Culture: Chinese Characters is written at invitation of China Intercontinental Press.

This book is written in simple words and plentiful pictures, and makes a brief introduction to the basic knowledge of great and profound Han character culture, which is designed to enable foreign friends to set foot on a relaxed and beneficial journey to the "Kingdom of Han Characters". I sincerely hope it can help its readers to get a general knowledge of and become interested in the Han character culture, thus improve their ability to recognize and use the Han characters, and play a role in Sino-foreign cultural exchanges.

Han characters are square graphic characters and the only ancient characters have being used up to now and called the "living fossils", which is regarded as a miracle in the history of human civilization.

Han characters originated from drawings. The forms of the Han characters evolved through Jiaguwen (inscriptions on animal bones or tortoise shells), Jinwen (inscriptions on ancient bronze ware), Xiaozhuan (the lesser seal style Chinese characters of the Qin Dynasty (221BC–206 BC)), Lishu (official script in the Han Dynasty (206 BC–220 AD), and Kaishu (regular script). Gradually drawings evolved into strokes, pictographic characters became symbols, and complex characters changed into simple ones. Simplification has always been the mainstream in the development of the Han characters. All these are covered in this book with plenty of statements and pictures.

As a kind of graphic written language, Han characters have unique intrinsic graphic feature and pictographic visual feature, which are highlighted throughout the book. As we know, modern Han characters are no longer pictographic characters but with unchanged graphic feature, and keep the forms of ancient pictographic characters to varying degrees. Fully exploring the dominant or recessive pictographic element in modern Han characters is of some value for recognition and use of Han characters.

As the "living fossils", Han characters have the square structure containing a wealth of information, concentrate civilization of the Chinese nation for thousands of years. The book also introduces and appreciates these heavy elements of Chinese culture, and Han characters' excellent performance as an art.

As the ancient characters used by the largest number of people in the world, Han characters themselves are still in development and bound to maintain their youth forever.

In brief:

Han characters

The written symbols of Chinese language

Han characters

Unique graphic characters

They date back to ancient times

Originate from drawings

They are notable and glamorous

Shoulder profound history

Progress in a thriving manner

They stride gorgeously forward

Constantly self-improve

Firmly self-perfect

Like a long river

Running forward with resounding songs

THE DAWN OF CIVILIZATION

Characters are the written symbols of language, and are the most important symbols of human civilization.

The first few characters appeared in what we call the River Civilization of some Oriental societies. Dating back to around 5,000 years ago, with a desire raised to communicate and record, ancestors living in these societies almost coincidentally kept track of their thoughts using drawing-like written symbols, which is a recording way generally accepted as being their original common choice.

Graphic Characters of the River Civilization

Human beings witnessed a great leap in their evolutionary history when they developed from no language to the emergence of language. And they subsequently witnessed another important leap forward when they progressed from no characters to the emergence of characters.

On Way to Civilization

Characters can be broadly categorized into two kinds: Graphic characters and alphabetic writing. The oldest characters, created in ancient Oriental nations, evolved from drawings, and therefore fall into the first category. About 5,500 years ago, the Sumerians living in the areas drained by the Tigris and Euphrates Rivers invented cuneiform characters on clay tablets. Some 5,000 years ago, the Egyptians living the Nile River Valley wrote pictographic characters on papyrus. Some 500 years later, the Indian ancients living in the Indus River Valley invented seal characters of their own. All of these belong to the category of pictographs. At the time between 5,000–3,000 years ago, the Chinese people living in the Yellow and Yangtze River Valleys wrote characters on pottery, tortoise shells and bones and bronze utensils, and these characters also belong to the pictographic category. These ancient characters demonstrated the exceptional intelligence of the River Civilizations. These earliest original ancient symbols as known

The cuneiform characters on clay tablets in early times were pictographic symbols.

Stele of the Code of Hammurabi. The stele is 2.25m high. The engraving on the upper part indicates that the Sun God is delivering a royal sceptre to the King Hammurabi. The lower part is the Law, inscribed in 8,000 cuneiform characters on clay tablets.

H.C. Rawlinson, a British scholar, made rubbings of cuneiform characters on clay tablets on the side of a steep cliff. Rawlinson subsequently took at least a dozen years to successfully break down all the cuneiform characters on the rock engraving, who is called "The Father of Cuneiform Characters on Clay Tablets".

to man, though not entirely documented the language, have condensed key messages of it.

Ancient Sumerian Cuneiform Characters

Cuneiform characters are generally accepted as being the earliest of their kind in the world. They were created by the Sumerians in Mesopotamia some 5,500 years ago. They were symbols impressed into clay tablets using pens which were actually reeds. The strokes of these characters are thick at one end and thin at the other, giving the impression of being wedges or nails. People of later generations called them cuneiform characters on clay tablets or T-shaped characters. The cuneiform characters on clay tablets evolved from drawings, belonging to the pictographic category mentioned above. The cuneiform characters on clay tablets were very popular during the Babylonian period. After some 3,000 years, they gradually died out. Today, some 2,000 years later, approximately 750,000 clay tablets with cuneiform characters have been found. In addition, many cuneiform characters have been found on mountainsides, as well as on stone tablets and pillars. The cuneiform characters representing the Code of Hammurabi on the pillars and the Behistun Inscriptions inscribed on pieces of stone wall are the most spectacular of all. Nevertheless, the cuneiform, with meanings that have been lost

long ago, have made European scholars being at sea for centuries.

Rawlison (1810–1859), a British scholar, decoded the Behistun Inscriptions inscribed on pieces of stone wall in 1851, unveiling the secrets of cuneiform characters. On 91-meter-high cliffs in Behistun village, the Behistun Inscriptions were inscribed with three languages, the upper part is Babylonian cuneiform, the middle part Elamite and the lower part ancient Persian. Rawlison started his efforts with ancient Persian, the most familiar one to him. The decoding of the Behistun Inscriptions makes it possible for people to have some understanding of the ancient civilization in the two river valleys. Otherwise, the brilliant ancient civilization will be buried in the dust of history forever.

Ancient Egyptian Pictographs

Some 5,000 years ago, ancient Egyptians living in the Nile River Valley created their pictographs, and these can still be seen on Egyptian pyramids, temples, stone objects and pottery. They inscribed these pictographs on a kind of papyrus, using reed pens, and bound them into rolls which subsequently became the world's most ancient books. In 525, when the Persians conquered the Egyptians, Egyptian pictographs that had existed for some 3,000 years died out. When the monk as the last person to understand the Egyptian pictographs passed away, their meaning became lost.

Pictographic Characters in Ancient Egypt

Ancient Egyptian pictographs had been covered by mysterious veils for a long time. In 1798, French troops of Napoléon Bonaparte (August 15, 1769–May 5, 1821) went on an expedition to Egypt. One year later, when French soldiers built the fortifications in Rosetta town at the mouth of the Nile, a piece of stone covered with carved inscriptions in ancient Egyptian pictographs, demotic pictographs and Greek characters, was discovered among the pile of rocks in a quarry. This is the famous Rosetta Stone. By virtue of Greek inscriptions, Champollion (1790–1832), a French genius scholar who is proficient in dozens of archaism, decoded the pictographs on the Stone in 1824. And then, the mysteries of ancient Egyptian pictographs were solved, with ancient Egyptian civilization revealed itself, contributing to the appearance of the "Egyptology".

Ancient Indian Harappa Seal Characters

Seal Characters in Ancient India. These mysterious symbols, engraved on a square seal, are obviously pictographic characters, and they are waiting quietly for their mysteries to be decoded.

Ancient India, one of the cradles of human civilization, made a uniquely original contribution to that civilization in the spheres of philosophy, literature, and natural science. The ancient civilization of India was rediscovered in the early part of the 20th century, specifically the Harappa Culture in the drainage areas of the Indus River. Harappa bronze-age culture emerged about 4,500 years ago and disappeared quite suddenly 800 years later. It existed at almost the same time as the Xia Dynasty (2070–1600 BC) in China. Archaeologists subsequently discovered the ruins of several cities, including Harappa, and some of these were of considerable size. They have even been called the "Manhattan of the Bronze-Ware Age". Archaeologists discovered characters from the Harappa period in the city ruins, inscribed on seals made of stone, pottery, or ivory and thus called "Seal Characters". More than 2,500 seals and over 500 character symbols have been discovered, and these symbols are mostly pictographic characters, although some are alphabetic writings. It is astonishing to find exquisite engravings of animal images on each small seal, and the artistic level is considerably high.

Different from Mesopotamian cuneiform characters and Egyptian pictographs, the seal characters of ancient India have not been translated. Furthermore, the Harappa Culture disappeared suddenly after an existence of only hundreds of years, so the seal characters, as well as ancient Harappa Culture itself, remain mysteries to philologists and historians. As for the

City Ruins of Harappa Culture. The cities of Harappa Culture that have been discovered in the drainage area of the Indus River are all of great size. Exquisite seal characters were discovered in the ruins of these cities.

well-known ancient Sanskrit, it emerged later and in all probability has no direct connection with the seal characters

Ancient Chinese Pictographs

China, one of the ancient civilized countries in the East, has a 5,000–year history of characters. Image symbols carved and painted on the potteries during the Dawenkou Culture in Shandong Province of the lower reach of the Yellow River, should be recognized as the earliest characters in China. While Jiaguwen inscribed on tortoise shells and animal bones some 3,000 years ago, on which the development of the later characters based, should be systematic and comparatively mature one. No less than the ancient characters created by other oriental civilizations, the character symbols in early China were so much like drawings, both using pictographic forms to express meanings.

Jiaguwen Recording Sacrificial Hunting

Different Fates of Graphic Characters of the River Civilization

A seafaring nation with a mysterious source, turned out to reverse the trend of graphic characters of at least two River civilizations.

The Creation of Alphabetic Characters

At the time between the 13th–11th century BC, there was a nation that good at seafaring and commercial activities, in the east coast of the Mediterranean (currently the areas of Syria and Lebanon). They were always dressed in bright purple robes and known as "the Phoenicians" (it means "purple" in Greek). In response to the need of bookkeeping in a faster and

Phoenicians Creating 22 Alphabets

more effective manner, resulting from the frequent communication in the spheres of business and seafaring, also in the light of Babylonian cuneiform and Egyptian pictographs, the Phoenicians created the simple Phoenician alphabet (including 22 alphabets), a sort of convenient and practical civilian characters.

On this basis, the Greeks created the Greek alphabet, from which the Latin alphabet coined in Roman Empire originated. But Sumerian cuneiform and ancient Egyptian pictographs, at the same time, gradually died out completely. Alphabetic characters combined with any language are likely to form a new kind of characters. Thus, so many different types of alphabetic characters emerged, in continents of Europe diversified in nationalities and languages. Europe was dotted with nationalities using various alphabetic, drawing the foreshadowing of the later formation of a state-lined political pattern. We can say that almost all phonetic alphabets of today's European countries evolved from the Greek and Latin one, also say that the characters of Phoenician alphabet is their ancestor.

Over the time, however, the graphic characters of ancient Egypt, Babylon and ancient India eventually disappeared or were replaced by alphabetic characters, which should be attributable to the fate of history.

The Only Living Ancient Characters

When it comes to China's pictographs, the fate becomes different. For Jiaguwen discovered in 1899, it only took Chinese scholars a couple of days to decode a lot of them, by dint of Jinwen (inscriptions on the bronze) in some similar fonts. This shows that Han characters have the same origin, representing the continuity of cultures, i.e., the previous ones are manifested in the later ones. It is this relationship that made the decoding of Jiaguwen unlike that of cuneiform or ancient Egyptian pictographs, which needed the aid of other characters.

In a word, different from the ancient characters of other civilizations which disappeared one by one, the Han characters have mysteriously endured, even up to the present day. In the strong atmosphere of Chinese culture, these characters have remained in use for generations of Chinese people. Regardless of changing Dynasties, the characters have undergone no substantial alteration; integrated with Chinese people's concrete thinking and realistic idea, they have tenaciously kept the quality of expressing meaning through structure. As a continuation of 5,000 years of Chinese history, the development of Han characters has never interrupted. Today, the Han characters have become the modern world's only living ancient characters, which should be a truly miracle in the history of human civilization.

The Yellow River Fostering Chinese Civilization

Common Choice of Graphic Ideograph

In order to express some simple meaning, no other way can be more direct and convenient than drawings. And it was only after a long time that drawings became further abstract and symbolized and eventually evolved into characters that could be enunciated as speech.

Rock Paintings for Recording Events

Drawings are the most direct and simplest way to express meaning. Long before the invention of characters, ancestors in the Eastern and Western primitive societies invariably recorded events using drawings engraved or painted on rocks, which were known as the rock paintings. Rock paintings, the earliest method to record events and oldest paintings in our history, represented the greatest artistic achievements in the Stone Age of primitive society. So far, they have been discovered in more than 120 countries and regions all around the world, like the famous cave paintings in Altamira in Spain and in Lascaux in France, as well as the rock paintings in many places of China, all vividly represent the old and mysterious primitive world. Surprisingly, some rock paintings 10,000 years ago show an extremely high level of painting art. It should be noted that many rock paintings in China had developed patterns and symbols, and others were similar to the pictographic characters of later times.

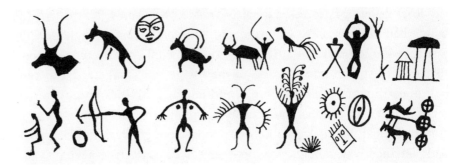

Ancient Rock-Painting Drawings in China. Many rock-painting drawings developed into specific patterns and were similar to pictographic characters. The drawings in the painting seem like the original forms of such pictographic characters as 牛 Niu(cattle), 犬 Quan (dog), 羊 yang (sheep), 牧 Mu (herding), 鸟 Niao (bird), 人 Ren (people), 射 She (shooting), 亦 Yi (armpit), 舞 Wu (dancing), 美 Mei (beauty), 女 Nu (female), 面 Mian (face), 日 Ri (sun), 宀 (a component of Han Characters), 木 Mu (wood), and 车 Che (vehicle).

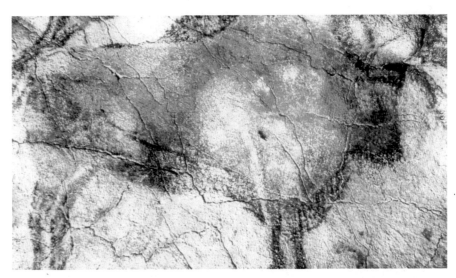

Cave Paintings in Altamira in Spain (Late Paleolithic Age). The shape is accurate and skillful, the strokes are bold and powerful, and the color is thick and intense. It is hard to believe that this masterpiece was created 10,000 years ago.

Rock paintings expressed a narrow range of meaning in artistic form, which had no relation to language and had no spoken equivalent. They just appeared on rocks of cliff or cavern and would not become symbols that widely spread information, so they were not characters. But rock paintings illustrated natural things and human activities and expressed meaning visually, and this was actually a way of recording events. It can be confirmed that, the rock paintings developed in a graphically ideographic and patterned way, though were not themselves characters, have played a role in the creation of later characters, at least pictographic characters. Thus, we can say that they were the abundant source of Han characters.

Pottery Paintings for Recording Events

When entering the Neolithic Age, pottery was fired in some ancient Eastern and Western civilizations, with simple and unvarnished paintings. As a brand new item, it was created by human using natural products according to their own will, for the first time. Undoubtedly, it is a symbol of the Neolithic Age.

During the age of the Yangshao Culture some 6,000 years ago, many drawings and decorative patterns painted on earthenware were produced in the areas drained by the Yellow River. These drawings and patterns are simple, unvarnished, artless, vivid and interesting, many of them enjoyed a very strong sense of decoration, and showed the painting skills of our ancient ancestors. As the drawings on the earthenware were colored in black, red and white, etc., these pottery items became known as "painted pottery". They are most numerous and most characteristic in the period of the Yangshao Culture, and we thus often refer to the Yangshao Culture as the "culture of painted pottery".

Just like the rock paintings, pottery paintings did not form symbols, had no relation with language, or pronunciation, or the role of spreading information, so they were not characters, only the excellent works of ancient art.

China's ancient rock paintings as well as pottery drawings and patterns revealed the achievements of the ancient art. Although they were not characters, their ideographic and patterned features have paved the way for the creation of pictographic characters.

Yangshao Culture

A culture emerged in the middle and lower reaches of the Yellow River at the Neolithic Age some 7,000 to 5,500 years ago. People at that time have settled down and knew how to fire the painted pottery, with production activities dominated by agriculture (among which millet was the main agricultural product) and supplemented with animal husbandry, fishing and hunting as well as gathering, etc. Some potteries during the age of Yangshao Culture were painted with beautiful drawings, these ideographic drawings have enlightened function on the invention of pictographic characters, while geometric symbols inscribed on the pottery were more closely with the creation of Han characters.

Colored Pottery Jar (Yangshao Culture Period). The work was created 6,000 years ago. Archaeologists thought the drawings recorded a war between ancient societies, where the clan with bird as totem conquered the clan with fish as totem.

ORIGIN OF HAN CHARACTERS

Han characters originated from drawings. In the early period of creating characters, Chinese people selected the way of expressing meaning by figures, and the creation of Han characters began with drawings.

Han characters are a form of ideographic visual symbols and originated from the vision of ancient Chinese people. It is a particular way of observing the world. Among various legends about the origin of Han characters, there is one story that is particularly widespread: Han characters were created by Cang Jie, who had four eyes.

Legends in Ancient Time

Various mysterious legends of ancient time
usually have some basis in historical reality.

Fu Xi Drew the Eight Diagrams

It is said that in the drainage area of the Yellow River in ancient times, Fu Xi, an obscure figure, taught people to make nets for fishing and showed them how to feed livestock, so people began to lead a life of fishing, hunting and animal husbandry. It is said Fu Xi drew the Eight Diagrams which resulted in the Han characters. The mysterious Eight Diagrams Fu Xi created were used for divination and are composed of the symbols "—" and "– –". "—" representing Yang and "– –" representing Yin. Yin and Yang go together, three couples constitute a group, and there are eight groups altogether. Each group is a divinatory symbol and has its own name, representing different natural phenomena and things, namely sky, earth, water, fire, wind, thunder, mountain and marsh. It is instructive to see that the Eight Diagrams are very far from the forms of Han characters. How did these long and short horizontal lines evolve into the Han characters with their abundant strokes and complex structures? It is sometimes hard to believe that the Eight Diagrams are the

Mystery Eight Diagrams.
Eight Diagrams contain
abundant ideological
contents and wisdom of
ancient Chinese people.

origin of Han characters. With careful study, you will find only the numeral symbols, and very few Han characters have a distinct relationship with the Eight Diagrams. For example, the form of the number three " 三 " looks a little similar to the figure of " 乾 (qián)" in the Eight Diagrams, " ☰ "; and the form of the ancient character for water (水) " 〵 " bears a certain resemblance to the figure of " 坎 (kan)" in the Eight Diagrams, " ☵ ". But it is hard to imagine there is any really close relationship between the forms of other Han characters and the Eight Diagrams. Therefore, we are reluctant to believe that the Han characters originated from the Eight Diagrams.

Fu Xi Temple. The Fu Xi Temple is situated in Tianshui City, Gansu Province. It is said that Fu Xi and Nv Wa, ancestors of the Chinese people, were born in this region.

Recording Events by Knots

Before the invention of characters, recording events by the use of knots was a very popular way of allowing primitive people to remember something of importance in their lives. And it played an important role in the life of ancient people. People made big knots on ropes for major events and small knots for those of lesser importance, and more events resulted in more knots. However, only those who made knots could understand these knots, which might help them remember something but were unable to function as a language. For example, ancient people made knots to record the prey that they caught. However, did the knot mean a deer, a wild boar or a goat? Only the person who made it could understand the exact meaning. Therefore, in terms of making knots, the function of recording events and information is poor while the scope of application is limited. And it couldn't perform as an effective way to widely spread information. That is, it is impossible to make Han characters just by using various forms of knots on lengths of rope. Academic research has led to the conclusion that some numerical symbols in the Han characters might have evolved from the knot symbols.

Ancient people recorded events by knots. They made knots to record the prey that they caught. However, only the person who made it could understand the exact meaning.

People made knots to record events, which was the same as the goal of creating characters. Therefore, the time of knots was not really so far away from the time of characters.

Cang Jie Created Characters

It is a popular and mysterious legend that Cang Jie created characters. More than 5,000 years ago the Yellow Emperor, ancestor of the Chinese people, united the areas drained by the Yellow River and established a huge clan-alliance of the local people. The Yellow Emperor had a historiographer named Cang Jie. Cang Jie was an amazing man. It is also said that he had four eyes, each of which could observe all the objects of the world. When he raised his head and watched the form of stars in the sky, and when he lowered his head and watched the tracks of birds and animals on

It is said that Cang Jie had four eyes.

the ground, he became enlightened and realized that different forms could distinguish different objects, so he created pictographic characters. What is even more astonishing is that, as recorded in Huai Nan Zi (a Chinese ancient book) "昔 xi 者 zhe 仓 cang 颉 jie 作 zuo 书 shu, 而 er 天 tian 雨 yu 粟 su, 鬼 gui 夜 ye 哭 ku", the gods were moved by the merit of Cang Jie in the creation of characters and granted the world rain of millet, but the ghosts, in fear of their secrets being revealed, cried all night. It appeared that the creation of Han characters was a major event that astonished the world and frightened the ghosts. Han characters held a very sacred position in the minds of these ancient people. And Cang Jie, the creator of Han characters, became the "God of Characters" admired by generations of Chinese people.

Implications from the Creation of Characters by Cang Jie

Today, such a marvelous thing is unbelievable. Also, the creation of Han characters solely by Cang Jie does not accord with the facts, since the creation of a set of standardized characters must surely have experienced a considerably long period of development. In fact, the Han characters were created collectively by the early Han people over a long period of laboring and living. Furthermore, if there was Cang Jie in ancient times, then he should be a very scholarly person who could sort out various characters.

The legend that Cang Jie created characters is of great value in exploring the origins of Han characters. The creation way adopted by Cang Jie, using four eyes to observe all the objects of the world, tells us this: Han characters are a form of ideographic visual symbols, and the creation of Han characters had its genesis in drawings.

Exploration of the Origination of Han Characters

Finding out the true origination of Han characters is significant to the study on the origination, evolution, development and application of Han characters. The archaeological findings are the only entrance we can access to the old age from when the Han characters dated.

Two Kinds of Pottery Carving and Painting Symbols

In ancient times the Chinese people carved and painted many symbols on pottery. These carved and painted symbols became the most important materials from which we are able to research the origin of Han characters. They principally consist of two kinds: the geometric and imagistic symbols.

Symbols Carved and Painted on Pottery Unearthed in Banpo, Xi'an

Symbols Carved and Painted on Pottery Unearthed in Erlitou

Geometric Symbols

Archaeologists have discovered many earthenware items with geometric symbols in the ruins of the Yangshao Culture in the middle reaches of the Yellow River, in such specific places as Banpo Village and Jiangzhai Village in Xi'an. These symbols, consisting of lines carved and painted on pottery about 5,000 to 6,000 years ago, are too simple and abstract, so it is hard to figure out their meaning or definitely say that, yes, they must be Han characters. But many of these symbols were repeated, which implies that they were carved and painted with serious intent, and must have had some function with regard to recording events. Recently, more than 20 kinds of carved and painted symbols made on items of pottery were discovered in Erlitou, Henan Province, dating back at least 4,000 years. The forms of the symbols were very similar to those on the earthenware excavated from

Totems or Clan Emblems on the Pottery and Bronze. It is believed by philologists that these symbols are the origins of such pictographic characters as 蛇 She (snake), 象 Xiang (elephant), 猪 Zhu (pig), 牛 Niu (cattle), 龙 Long (dragon), 虎 Hu (tiger), 犬 Quan (dog), 羊 Yang (sheep), 鹿 Lu (deer), 鸟 Niao (bird), 鱼 Yu (fish), 月 Yue (moon), 日 Ri (sun), 山 Shan (mountain), 火 Huo (fire), and 美 Mei (beauty).

Banpo and Jiangzhai villages, and some of them bore a close similarity to the Jiaguwen of the Shang and Zhou Dynasties.

We cannot say for certain that these geometric symbols are actually characters, but this kind of line structure was consistent with the Han characters that were developed later. What we can say, however, is that the geometric carved and painted symbols on the pottery of the Yangshao Culture are probably the origin of the Han characters.

Image Symbols

About 5,000 years ago, people who lived near Taishan Mountain, Shandong carved and painted image symbols on the pottery to record events or as totems, which are the famous Dawenkou Culture Carved and Painted Symbols on the Pottery. These image symbols, which describe things by lines, were obviously different from geometric symbols, and seem like the Jiaguwen inscriptions on bones or tortoise shells of a later time. We find the same symbol in many places, even in a thousand miles away, which implies that this symbol not only had the function of spreading information but was also in frequent usage and might have some sort of pronunciation. Therefore, it is believed by many expert scholars that these image symbols carved and painted during the Dawenkou Culture, which had form, meaning and pronunciation, should be recognized as the earliest characters in China: the original image characters.

Let's see an image symbol carved on earthenware. This symbol looks like a drawing representing the morning: the sun rises over lofty mountains, pierces through the clouds, and slowly illuminates the world below. It is morning. Many philologists say that this is

Dawenkou Culture

A culture at the Neolithic Age some 6,000 to 4,500 years ago, mainly generated in northern Shandong, Jiangsu, Anhui and other places in the lower reaches of the Yellow River. During which the early period was dominated by a matriarchal clan commune system, while the middle and later periods led by a patriarchal one. At that time, farming has become the major production activities. With the pottery-making technologies at a high level, there were black and white potteries, including some carved with image symbols. Image symbols carved and painted on the earthenware of the Dawenkou Culture are probably the earliest characters in China.

the character of " 旦 dan" (meaning dawn). " 旦 dan" means dawn. The upper part " 日 " is the sun and the lower part " 一 " is the simplification of mountains and clouds. Does this symbol of " 旦 " carved on earthenware represent the sun-rise that Dawenkou people would often see over the Taishan Mountain? The symbol of " 旦 " was found in Shandong, Anhui and Jiangsu, which meant it not only spread information, but also might have some sort of pronunciation. In addition, many philologists also say that this symbol of " 旦 " was a clan totem, which is also perfectly reasonable, because according to studies of the Han characters, many image clan totems or clan emblems were incorporated into the characters of a later time.

Generally in terms of the development, Han characters are divided into three distinct stages by philologists, i.e., the primitive drawing-like

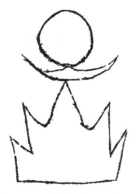

Pottery of the Dawenkou Culture and Symbol of 旦 (Dan) Carved on It

Sun-rising on the Taishan Mountain. Dawenkou people in ancient times often saw this charming sun-rising scene.

characters, ancient characters and modern characters. These image symbols carved and painted on the earthenware of the Dawenkou Culture that considered by many philology experts as "characters", should be classified into the first stage, during which they were similar to drawings and few, well short of the Han characters system. Nevertheless, it indicated that, with the frequent appearance and maturity in the near future, Han characters were about to enter the second stage.

Damaidi Rock-Painting Drawing Symbols. Recently, intensive ancient rock-painting cluster has been discovered in Damaidi, Zhongwei, Ningxia Province. There are more than 1,500 individual paintings with patterns and symbols, some of which are similar to graphic characters. (Picture selected from Discover the Rock Paintings, Li Xiangshi)

Supposition of the Time of the Origination of Han Characters

The generation of Han characters has experienced a long period of time. The ancient legend that Cang Jie created characters, the pictographic ideograph of rock paintings and painted pottery, the image carving symbols had the ideogram, as well as totems and clan badges have informed us that drawings were the main source of Han character, in other words, Han characters originated from drawings. On ancient pottery the geometric carving symbols had the structure of lines and the image carving symbols had the ideogram, which were the important features of the Han characters that would be developed later. In this case, we can date Han characters to about the period of the Yangshao Culture approximately 6,000 years ago. Image symbols during the Dawenkou Culture, the earliest group of Han characters, appeared in the foot of the Taishan Mountain in Shandong Province of the lower reach of the Yellow River around 5,000 years ago. Of course, this supposition requires a greater degree of excavated proof. In short, the formation of Chinese characters has certainly experienced a slow and long process of development.

In recent years, new archaeological findings concerning the origination of Han characters have provided relevant exploration with important data, such as Damaidi rock paintings in Zhongwei, Ningxia, carving symbols on tortoise shells in Jiahu, Henan, etc., inspiring infinite imaginations of us on the origination of Han character once again.

Carving Symbols on Tortoise Shells in Jiahu, Henan

In 1987, when archaeologists carried out an excavation at the Jiahu Site in the upper reaches of the Huaihe River, a piece of tortoise shell was unearthed in a grave. It was inscribed with a symbol in the shape of " 目 mu (eye)" , much like the Jiaguwen " 目 mu (eye)" founded in the Yin's Ruins. Coupled with another 17 carving symbols on tortoise shells, stone objects and potteries, it caused a sensation in academia. The Jiahu Site is originated from the Neolithic Age, if these symbols are recognized as characters, the origination should be traced back to 8,000 years ago. This means that not only the time of origination of the Han characters needs to be re-examined, also the history of the world's ancient characters shall be re-written. On the contrary, even these symbols on tortoise shells are not characters themselves, they should be the world's oldest carving symbols, offering vital clues for the exploration of the origination of Han characters.

有4条墓道的王陵墓
M1002
横排. Han.

EVOLVEMENT OF FORMS OF HAN CHARACTERS

The evolution of the Han characters underwent a very long course of development. In the period of more than 3,000 years from Jiaguwen inscriptions on bones or tortoise shells of the Shang Dynasty to Kaishu (regular script) of today, the forms of the Han characters evolved through Jiaguwen, Jinwen (inscriptions on ancient bronze ware), Xiaozhuan (the lesser seal style Chinese characters of the Qin Dynasty (221–206 BC)), Lishu (official script in the Han Dynasty (206 BC–220 AD), and Kaishu. Gradually drawings evolved into strokes, pictographic characters became symbols, and complex characters changed into simple ones. Simplification has always been the mainstream in the development of the Han characters.

Ancient Drawing-like Characters

After the stage of "primitive drawing characters" , Han characters entered a new phase of "ancient characters" . These characters still looked to some degree like drawings, but were comparatively mature. The mature Han characters indicated that China has progressed from an era of shadowy legend into a time of true history.

Characters from Underground – Jiaguwen

Some 100 years ago, when the local farmers in Xiaotun Village, Anyang, Henan Province worked in the fields, they often found some fragments of bone in the soil. They converted these into a traditional Chinese medicine named "longgu" (dragon's bones) and sold them in pharmacies for a little extra money. These dragon's bones are actually Jiagu, which refers to tortoise shells and bones. And the symbols inscribed on them are Jiaguwen inscriptions on bones or tortoise shells; they have been quietly sleeping underground for more than 3,000 years.

Jiaguwen is a kind of character of the Shang (1600–1046 BC) and Western Zhou (1046–771 BC) Dynasties. Such characters are an integration of form, pronunciation and meaning. They could be used to record each word in spoken language, and there also appeared phrases and simple sentences. Jiaguwen was a kind of ideographic symbolic language that

A Piece of Tortoise Shell Carved with Characters (Shang Dynasty, unearthed in Yin's Ruins)

Yin's Ruins

Yin's Ruins, located in what we now know as Xiaotun Village, Anyang, Henan Province, was the capital of the Shang Dynasty 3,000 years ago and was also the earliest settled capital in China's history. In 1300 BC the 20th king of the Shang Dynasty, Pan Geng, moved the capital to Yin, and it remained so until the dynasty's end. More than 80 palaces and ancestral temple ruins, plus 14 grand imperial graves, have been excavated from Yin's Ruins, and abundant cultural relics of the Shang Dynasty have been unearthed, including examples of Jiaguwen, bronze ware, jade, pottery, ornamental stone, lacquer ware, and textiles. In total, more than 100,000 pieces of Jiaguwen have been discovered. In July 2006 Yin's ruins were included in the list of the World Cultural Heritages.

could be pronounced and used to record complex ideas; also it consisted of comparatively mature characters. What a pity that for such a long time so many rare and ancient characters had been ground up and eaten as traditional Chinese medicine!

Discovery from TCM

Chinese people didn't realize the existence of Jiaguwen for thousands of years. In 1899, an official named Wang Yirong (1845–1900), who was in charge of wine sacrifice in the Imperial College of the Qing Dynasty (1616–1911), became sick and had to take traditional Chinese medicine. He found many very tiny inscriptions on the "dragon's bones" that had been bought. He was wild with joy and brought some bigger "dragon's bones". Wang Yirong was fond of ancient characters and was also a learned person. After the collection and study of the bones, he

Many scholars thought, except Wang Yirong of Beijing, Wang Xiang and Meng Dingsheng of Tianjing were also the people who discovered, collected and studied the first batch of Jiaguwen at the same time. The time that they found Jiaguwen was also 1899.

realized that the symbols on the bones were the very ancient characters from the Shang Dynasty (1600–1046 BC). These characters were inscribed on tortoise shells and animal bones, so people of later generations called them "Jiaguwen" (inscriptions on tortoise shells or bones). These Jiaguwen pieces came from Xiaotun Village, Anyang, Henan Province. The region around Xiaotun Village was the capital of the Shang Dynasty (1600–1046 BC), called "Yin". After the fall of the Shang Dynasty (1600–1046 BC), the area gradually fell into ruin and was eventually submerged, so people referred to the place as "Yinxu" (meaning, the ruins of the Yin). Hundreds and thousands of Jiaguwen pieces were dug out by farmers from the Yin's ruins. Now 150,000 pieces of Jiaguwen of the later Shang Dynasty (1600–1046 BC) have been unearthed from Yinxu and other places. More than 4,500 different character symbols have been discovered, and more than 1,500 characters have been interpreted.

Mysterious Divination

The society of the Shang Dynasty (1600–1046 BC) was possessed with the worship of gods and ghosts. The Emperor of the Shang Dynasty (1600–1046 BC) would make divination by tortoise shells and animal bones on whether there would be a harvest, if the wind and rain would be moderate or heavy, whether or not they would be victorious in war, or if they would be successful in hunting. They believed that heavenly gods and ancestral gods would give them inspiration. In the act of divination, they dug out some small round holes on the back of tortoise shells or animal bones, an official in charge would cry out and ask the heavenly gods and ancestral gods to settle the questions imposed by the emperor of the Shang Dynasty (1600–1046 BC), and fired or baked the small round holes on the back of the tortoise shells or animal bones with a red-hot charcoal stick. After heating, the tortoise shells and animal bones would crack. On the basis of the crack formed on the upper side, they would decide whether it was fortunate or unfortunate for the issue in question. If it was fortunate, they

Jiaguwen with Thin, Rigid and Straight Lines (Divination on Cattle Bones of Shang Dynasty)

would go ahead and do it, and if it was not, they would refrain. At last, they would inscribe the issues in question and the divination result on the tortoise shells and animal bones by characters and these characters were divination words, i.e. the Jiaguwen we find today. It can be said that Jiaguwen is a form of divination characters and these characters act as a sort of communication between man and god. Of course, there were a few Jiaguwen pieces used for recording events instead of divination.

Drawings Called Vigorous Lines

Jiaguwen was a kind of ancient character-language, but based on drawings. There were many pictographic characters that could manifest the typical features of things. For example, in Jiaguwen the characters of "(鹿) deer" and "(虎)tiger" could be written in various ways, but all drew the deer with horns and the tiger with stripes. In Jiaguwen the character of "(马) horse" must draw the mane on the horse's neck. The formal structure of a Jiaguwen character was basically composed of lines and strokes. Tortoise shells and animal bones are hard, and it is difficult

Examples of Common Jiaguwen

to inscribe characters on them, so the strokes of Jiaguwen were mostly straight lines carved with the point of a knife. The lines were thin, rigid and straight, and the curves were mostly square to show the beauty of primitive simplicity and vigorousness.

Jiaguwen, drawings composed of lines, had become a kind of indicative symbols, and people could understand their meanings. A large number of ideographic divination words on the tortoise shells and animal bones tell us that as early as in the Shang Dynasty (1600–1046 BC) more than 3,000 years ago, Han characters had become a comparatively complete system for recording language.

Multitude Working in Fields, Divination on Cattle Bones. It recorded the cultivation methods of agriculture of Shang Dynasty — the slaves were forced to conduct the farming in group in the fields of the emperor of Shang Dynasty.

Solar and Lunar Eclipse Cattle Bone. There are two lines of divination characters craved in this damaged cattle bone, which are interpreted as saying: "solar and lunar eclipse." Many scholars thought it was the record of solar eclipse in late Shang Dynasty, which took placed in 1200 BC.

History and Culture

Jiaguwen inscriptions on animal bones or tortoise shells had recorded the rich social life about the Shang Dynasties (1600–1046 BC), including agriculture, animal husbandry, sacrifice, wars, astronomy and daily life. For example, the famous divination on cattle bones, Multitude Working in Fields, of the Shang Dynasty (1600–1046 BC) principally tells the story about the emperor of the Shang Dynasty (1600–1046 BC), who asked god, "If the emperor orders a multitude of people to work together in the fields, can we get a good harvest?" These divination characters reflect the fact that farming in the Shang Dynasty (1600–1046 BC) was conducted by slaves in groups. The Moon Eclipse Again, characters on cattle bones of the Shang Dynasty (1600–1046 BC) with great scientific value, are interpreted as saying: "Renyin Zhen Moon Eclipse Again (壬寅贞月又食)." According to specialists, it was the written record of a total lunar eclipse, which occurred on the second day of the seventh month of 1173 BC. Jiaguwen had record many natural phenomena, such as lunar eclipse, solar eclipse, heavy rain, rainbow, gale, drought, sand storm. The historical facts of Shang Dynasty basically conformed to Shi Ji (Records of the Grand Historian) written by later historian Sima Qian (145–87 BC). It not only confirmed the existence of Shang Dynasty (1600–1046 BC), but also confirmed that Records of the Grand Historians is a credible historical works. And that is very important.

Mystery of Fu Hao

In 1976 archaeologists excavated a medium royal grave of the Shang Dynasty (1600–1046 BC) in the palace area in Xiaotun Village, Anyang, in which there were 1,928 pieces of bronze and jade objects buried together with the dead person. The grave master was a woman named "Fu Hao". Who is Fu Hao? There is not a single record in any ancient books. But archaeologists were nevertheless filled with excitement. They lost no time in telling each other, "We have found Fu Hao! We have found Fu Hao!" In fact the name "Fu Hao" had appeared many times in Jiaguwen characters, and at least 200 pieces of tortoise shell or animal bone had recorded her. She was the wife of Wu Ding, Emperor of the Shang Dynasty (1600–1046 BC) and was a brave and beautiful female general. She had led the army to defeat the enemy for many times. She held palace sacrificial ceremonies and divinations many times and had a very high position and was accorded corresponding prestige. Jiagu divination words disclose a story both sweet and sad. Wu Ding constantly cared about the welfare of Fu Hao with the battle still raging outside the castle walls, worried about everything regarding her, and made divination for her health and safety almost every day, "now it is rainy in the north, does she know how to pay attention to the weather?" "It is cold these days, will she feel the cold?" "She has a pain in her bones; oh, how about her now?" The short-verse divination words on the tortoise shells and animal bones were full of Wu Ding's profound thoughts and endless love for Fu Hao. Later Fu Hao died, at the age of 33. Wu Ding was overwhelmed with sadness. He buried his beloved wife within the palace walls, and held a ceremonious funeral. Jiaguwen revealed the story of Fu Hao and revealed a touching love story of the Shang Dynasty (1600–1046 BC) 3,000 years ago, which can still bring a tear to the eye.

" 婦好 (Fu Hao)" Carved in Tortoise Shells. "Fu Hao" has appeared more than 240 times in Tortoise shells.

Brave and Beautiful Female General of Shang Dynasty – Fu Hao

Wonder of Bronze Ware Culture in the World
– Inscriptions on Bronze

In about 3,500 BC the East entered the Bronze Age. At that time the earliest bronze ware appeared in Mesopotamia and Egypt. The "Age of Bronze Ware" in China emerged a little later, in about 3,000 BC. During the Shang (1600–1046 BC) and Zhou (1046–256 BC) periods of the slavery society, the foundry of bronze ware in China reached its peak and this period was the real "Bronze Age" in China. The bronze ware of the Shang (1600–1046 BC) and Zhou (1046–256 BC) Dynasties became the wonder of the contemporary world by virtue of its beautiful shapes, exquisite line

Bronze Elephant Statue with
Exquisite Line Decorations
(Shang Dynasty)

decorations, superb craftsmanship and majestic inscriptions.

Bronze ware was based on bronze itself and a little tin, and had a beautiful sheen. At that time, bronze was called "Jin", so the inscriptions on the bronze ware items are called as "Jinwen" with "wen" meaning "inscriptions". Ding tripod and Zhong (bell) had the highest position in the sacrificial bronze vessels, and were represented by the most characters, so such characters are also known as "Zhong Ding Wen ". A large number of inscriptions appeared on Chinese bronze ware, which is a peculiar phenomenon in the bronze culture of the world.

Sacrificial Vessels Buried Underground

Bronze ware was a precious thing in the Shang (1600–1046 BC) and Zhou (1046–256 BC) Dynasties. It could be used as a container, and most often, and most importantly, it served as the sacrificial vessels of slave owners and nobles for their heavenly and earthly gods and ancestors. At that time, bronze ware had become the symbol of power, position and hierarchy. A person with a higher position possessed more bronze ware. For example, the bronze Ding tripod was one of the most important sacrificial vessels in the entire country. A king had the most, i.e. nine pieces, and other officials and nobles only had seven, five, three or one pieces, and common people

Simuwu Bronze Ding and Its Inscriptions (Shang Dynasty)

The inscription of 32 characters on Ligui of Western Zhou Dynasty revealed the secret of the time of "herding a field battle".

could not have any Ding. At that time princes and nobles often inscribed great events such as sacrifice, battle achievements, awards, and trade of slaves on the bronze ware in a style like Jiaguwen characters and intended for permanent preservation and memory, which is the Jinwen (inscriptions on the bronze). After the death of a prince or a noble, people would bury their bronze ware together with the dead. The bronze ware of the Shang (1600–1046 BC) and Zhou (1046–256 BC) that we can see today has almost all been excavated from burial sites.

Majestic Jinwen

The bronze ware of the Shang (1600–1046 BC) and Zhou (1046–256 BC) Dynasties had been unearthed as early as the Han Dynasty (206 BC–220 AD) and tens of thousands of various bronze ware items have been excavated right up until the present time. More than 3,000 different Jinwen characters were discovered on the bronze ware of the Shang (1600–1046 BC) and Zhou (1046–256 BC) Dynasties, and more than 2,000 have been decoded. Jinwen still looked like drawings. But on the whole the appearance of Jinwen was more shapely than that of Jiaguwen, the strokes were fuller and more rounded, the linear features had become stronger and stronger, and many characters were more simplified. In particular, Jinwen was first written by using

a brush, and then inscribed on the bronze ware, which was significantly different from the Jiaguwen, which was carved with a knife. Jinwen exhibited the writing effects of brushes and offered an aesthetic feeling of primitive simplicity, vigor and majesty.

Appearance of Long Inscriptions

In the Shang Dynasty (1600–1046 BC) the inscriptions on the bronze ware had very few characters and some even had only a couple of characters. For example, the Simuwu Ding of the Shang Dynasty (1600–1046 BC) unearthed from Yin's ruins weighs 832 kg. Inside the largest bronze Ding in ancient China there inscribed only three characters "Simuwu 司母戊 " which shows that this big bronze article was cast by Wu Ding, Emperor of the Shang Dynasty (1600–1046 BC), for holding sacrificial ceremony for his mother "Wu". In the Shang Dynasty (1600–1046 BC) the longest inscription had 42 characters. In the Western Zhou Dynasty (1046–771 BC) the inscriptions became longer. There appeared inscriptions of hundreds of characters on bronze ware, recording things in great detail. For example, on the Maogong Ding of the Western Zhou Dynasty (1046–771 BC) with the longest inscription, there are 497 characters which together compose a long passage. It is followed by the Sanshi Plate of the Western Zhou Dynasty (1046–771BC). A total of 357 characters were inscribed on its underside. As of the time of writing, the longest discovered passage of ancient China is the inscription on the bronze ware of the Western Zhou Dynasty (1046–771BC).

Historical Value of Inscriptions

At present, most important social and historical information regarding the Shang (1600–1046 BC) and Zhou (1046–256BC) Dynasties have been obtained from the inscriptions on the bronze ware. In 1976 a Ligui, a kind of bronze ware of the early Western Zhou Dynasty (1046–771 BC) was unearthed. Its inscription of 32 characters revealed a great deal about the occasion of "herding a field battle" by means of which the Emperor Wuwang of the Zhou Dynasty (1046–256 BC) conquered the Emperor Zhou of the Shang Dynasty (1600–1046 BC). It clearly tells us that this vital battle was finished within a day, which confirms the records in Shi Ji (Records of the Grand Historian) that "On the Day of Jiazi, the forces of the Shang Dynasty were defeated." The famous Dayu Ding has an inscription of 291 characters, recording a story about a nobleman named Yu of the Western Zhou Dynasty (1046–771 BC). He was commended by Emperor Zhou and the emperor told him with sincere words and earnest wishes that he would better not idle away his life in pleasure-seeking like the Emperor of the Shang Dynasty and should rather put his best efforts into serving his

Maogong Ding of the Western Zhou Dynasty is the bronze ware with the longest inscription in ancient China, which is carved with 497 characters.

Exquisite Shiqiang Plate (Western Zhou Dynasty)

country. On the Shiqiang Plate, a bronze ware of the Western Zhou Dynasty (1046–771 BC), the 284 characters on the reverse side praise the merits of all the past emperors of the Zhou Dynasty and tell the history of the maker's own family, from which we can learn a great deal, about the historical situation of the Western Zhou Dynasty (1046–771 BC) and the policies adopted by the Zhou Dynasty (1046–256 BC) regarding the survivors of the Shang Dynasty (1600–1046 BC), all of which boast a very high historical value.

The Jinwen of the Shang (1600–1046 BC) and Zhou (1046–256 BC) Dynasties formed a connecting link between the preceding Jiaguwen and the following Xiaozhuan (the lesser seal style adopted in the Qin Dynasty (221–206 BC)). Jinwen looked like drawings, but the characters had made a truly significant progress from pictographic and ideographic forms to the square linear ideographic words we recognize today.

Ancient Artistic Characters
– Xiaozhuan

Xiaozhuan (the lesser seal style of Chinese characters) was the result of the policy of "writing in same characters" adopted by Emperor Qinshihuang of the Qin Dynasty (221–206 BC). The forms of Xiaozhuan were simpler and the composition of lines was less similar to drawings. The emergence of Xiaozhuan marked the end for the ancient Chinese characters.

Figure of Emperor Qingshihuang

The Emergence of Xiaozhuan

During the Eastern Zhou Dynasty (770–256 BC) after Western Zhou Dynasty, the royal authority of Zhou Dynasty had collapsed, and the hereditary fiefs eventually became powerful in their own right. Especially in the Warring States Period (475–221BC), various states fought for hegemony and resulted in endless wars. In this context, the Han characters were not standardized and there were many variant forms. For each character, the 齐 Qi, 楚 Chu, 燕 Yan, 韩 Han, 赵 Zhao, and 魏 Wei States in the east and the 秦 Qin State in the west would have different ways of writing it, and the pronunciation of some characters was also different. In 221 BC, Ying Zheng, King of Qin state, conquered the six eastern states and united China, who called himself "Emperor Qinshihuang." In order to spread government orders to the whole nation and make people understood, Emperor

The Characters " 马 " and " 安 " in Various States in Warring States Period

Qinshihuang took immediate action to unify characters and instigated a nationwide policy of "writing in same characters". Emperor Qinshihuang ordered his Prime Minister Li Si to oversee the work of unifying characters. Using the characters prevalent in the Qin State as a standard, Li Si incorporated the advantages of the variant characters of all the states, and established a unified written language, i.e. Xiaozhuan. Zhuan means drawing with crooked lines. As Jiaguwen, Jinwen and the characters of the Warring States Period (475–221 BC) were always collectively known as Dazhuan (big seal characters), the characters unified by Emperor Qinshihuang of the Qin Dynasty (221–206 BC), which were simpler than Dazhuan in respect of their structure, were called Xiaozhuan (lesser seal characters).

Emperor Qinshihuang

Emperor Qinshihuang, named Ying Zheng (259–210 BC), was the king of the Qin State in the west. Later he spent ten years in conquering the six states in the east, ultimately uniting China in 221 BC, and subsequently established the first feudalist centralized country in its history. Emperor Qinshihuang was the first emperor of China. To safeguard the consolidation of the country, Emperor Qinshihuang adopted a policy of tyrannical domination. Meanwhile, he was responsible for many events of great historical importance. Besides unifying characters, scales of length, capacity and weight, and thought (burning books and burying Confucian scholars alive), he also built the Great Wall, laid roads, dug irrigation systems, fixed the unified sizes of carriages, and established counties (administrative regions), all of which had enormous influence over later generations.

Emperor Qinshihuang unified characters and established Xiaozhuan, which was the first large-scale simplification and standardization of Han characters, and basically established a single set of Han characters during the Warring States Period (475–221 BC).

Ancient Artistic Characters

Xiaozhuan is basically a very beautiful style of calligraphy. It owes this beauty to the ordered rectangular forms, regular and symmetric structure, rounded and graceful strokes, and lines with even thickness. Xiaozhuan consists of the most beautiful characters in ancient China and can truly be called the "artistic characters". Compared to Dazhuan, Xiaozhuan is simpler, and each single character has only one written form. In respect of strokes, the right-angles of Dazhuan became more rounded. The number of strokes and the forms and position of character components were also

Xiaozhuan with Beautiful Forms

fixed. And there appeared more components indicating sound and more pictophonetic characters with pronunciation and meaning. If you observe carefully, you will find occasional pictographic clues in the forms of some Xiaozhuan characters, but these features are not obvious, which indicates that Xiaozhuan has largely moved away from drawing.

Official Style of Characters in the Qin Dynasty (221–206 BC)

In the Qin Dynasty (221–206 BC) Xiaozhuan was the official style of character and it was used for all the important documents of the government. For example, when Emperor Qinshihuang standardized the scales of

Bronze Tiger-shaped Tally (Qing Dynasty). The Xiaozhuan on tiger-shaped tally has neat and symmetric forms.

length, capacity and weight, the inscriptions on the bronze imperial edicts issued across the country were in style of Xiaozhuan. Today we can see the imperial edict inscribed in the style of Xiaozhuan on many instruments of weight and measurement from the Qin Dynasty that have been unearthed all around China. We can also find the Xiaozhuan of the Qin Dynasty on the excavated coins, eaves tiles, weapons, tiger-shaped tallies (the tallies emperor used to mobilize army), and ancient steles of the Qin Dynasty.

Carving Stones of the Qin Dynasty (221–206 BC)

In 219 BC, having united China, Emperor Qinshihuang led a caravan of carts and horses and visited seven places, setting up a stone stele praising his merits at each of them. The inscriptions on these steles were written by Li Si in style of Xiaozhuan. The Xiaozhuan characters on the carved stones of the Qin Dynasty had an ordered and precise structure, with rounded and beautiful strokes, and a simple and vigorous style, and are viewed as the orthodox school of Xiaozhuan. Of the seven steles, only the Taishan Carved Stone and Langyatai Carved Stone are still extant, and most original stone inscriptions have been destroyed. We do actually have the other five carved stones, such as the Yishan Carved Stone, but these are later imitations. Carving Stones of the Qin Dynasty are the important materials of the development history of Han characters.

Rubbings of Taishan Carved Stone by Emperor Qinshihuang. The carved stone is kept in Dai Temple, Tai'an, Shandong Provience.

53

Modern Characters Dissimilar to Drawings

In the Qin Dynasty (221–206 BC), when scholars with lowly positions wrote Xiaozhuan (the lesser seal style) characters rapidly on thin strips of bamboo and wood, they could not have imagined that a whole new style of calligraphy was being created under their hands, i.e. Lishu (official script). The emergence of Lishu was a major event in the development of Han characters, which were no longer "ancient characters" and had begun to enter a new phase of "modern characters".

Great Changes in Forms of Han Characters

After Xiaozhuan, Han characters entered the stage of "modern characters" and the calligraphy styles included Lishu (official script) and Kaishu (regular script). From Lishu, the forms of Han characters totally broke away from drawing and became characters composed of strokes and symbols. There are more pictophonetic characters with pronunciation and meaning. Characters are no longer pictographs but indicative symbols. And the evolution from pictographic to indicative symbols marks a great change in the form of Han script and has an enormous significance in the history of Chinese characters.

Demarcation Line between Ancient and Modern Characters – Lishu

In the Qin Dynasty (221–206 BC), while Xiaozhuan was popular, another faster and more convenient style of calligraphy had found favor among the ordinary people, i.e. Lishu. During the Han Dynasty (206 BC–220 AD) Lishu developed its completely mature form. The structures of Lishu characters are composed of straight strokes and the forms are simplified. The characters are totally dissimilar to drawings and have been transformed into pure symbols. Thereafter, the Han characters were standardized. Lishu broke the pictographic mould of ancient characters, ending the ancient-character phase and ushering in the modern-characters we see today.

Contribution Made by Yamen Servants

Paper was invented during the Western Han Dynasty (206 BC–25 AD) and not widely adopted until the end of the Eastern Han Dynasty

Heicheng Ruins in Juyan. Since 1930s, many bamboo and wood strips of Han Dynasty have been unearthed from here.

Bamboo Strips of Lishu Unearthed in Wuwei, Gansu (Han Dynasty)

(25–220). In the Qin Dynasty (221–206 BC) and the Warring States Period (475–221 BC), therefore, people usually wrote characters on strips of bamboo or wood, using brushes. In order to write more quickly, the yamen servants who were in charge of composing official documents, adopted the calligraphy style prevalent among the ordinary folk, changing the rounded strokes of Xiaozhuan (the lesser seal style) similar to drawing to straight lines, and simplifying the forms, so that they were able to write very fast. This style of new, simplified calligraphy was created by lowly officials (Li people) whose job was to write documents, so people called it Lishu with "shu" meaning "writing". We can be quite certain that the use of brush pens and the accelerated writing of Xiaozhuan created Lishu, a kind of new style. We can find examples of this on many excavated bamboo and wooden strips, such as those of the Qin State from Shuihudi, Yunmeng. The forms of the Lishu characters on these strips were totally different from Xiaozhuan. More than 30,000 pieces of the famous Juyan Han strips have been revealed

Wood Strips of Han Dynasty in Juyan

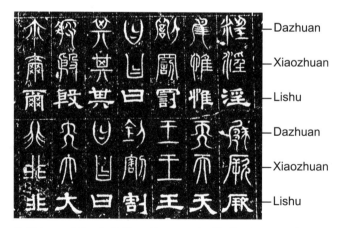

Rubbings of *Santi Shijing*. Compared with Dazhuan and Xiaozhuan, it is obvious that the forms of Lishu are dissimilar to drawing.

in Ejin River Basin, Inner Mongolia and the oblate Lishu characters on the Han examples not only show the superb level of Lishu calligraphy during the Han Dynasty (206 BC–220 AD), but also disclose the writers' liberty and relaxation. According to archaeological evidence, Lishu was a popular calligraphy style during the Qin Dynasty (221–206 BC), and only the important official documents needed to be written by Xiaozhuan. In the Han Dynasty (206 BC–220 AD) Lishu was in common use across the board, from government officials to ordinary people.

Change of Lishu – Great Revolution of Characters

Lishu was a great simplification of the strokes and forms of Xiaozhuan characters. The forms and structures composed of strokes and indicating symbols made the remnants of the pictographic lines in Xiaozhuan characters obsolete, and Han characters became ideographic symbols composed of strokes. It can be concluded that Lishu had become the demarcation line between the ancient and modern characters. That is, before Lishu, Han characters were "ancient characters" similar to drawings, and with the arrival of Lishu, Han characters became "modern characters" dissimilar from drawings. The evolution from Zhuanshu to Lishu in Han characters is known as the "Change of Lishu". After the change of Lishu, the lines of Han characters altered from bent to straight, the features of pictographic characters disappeared, and the characters began to take on a new style totally composed of strokes. We can say, in short, that a kind of drawing-like "line characters" changed to a kind of "stroke characters" entirely dissimilar to drawing. Thereafter, Han characters no longer resembled drawings. They had a far greater quality of symbolization, and were also simpler. People now found it much easier to learn and write Han characters. Change of Lishu was an enormous revolution in Han characters and had an epoch-making significance.

The Emergency of Han Li

"Han Li" is a kind of Lishu appeared in the Han Dynasty (206 BC–220 AD), which is able to be written fast in oblate forms.

To write faster on strips of bamboo and wood, the strokes became more flat and straight than those of the rounded Xiaozhuan, with some long ones disconnected, forming the stroke of point (、), horizontal (一), vertical (丨), left-falling (丿) and right-falling (㇏). A horizontal stroke has three turns within a wave, the endings of a horizontal, left-falling, and right-falling stroke rise upward, and the left-falling and right-falling strokes extend on two sides. The lively and beautiful wave-like strokes are the most obvious features of Han Li. In addition, to write more characters on strips of bamboo and wood, made the Lishu characters much more oblate than Xiaozhuan characters, with the form and structure more simplified. For example, the components of " 水 shui (water)" , " 手 shou (hand)" and

Many various strokes in Xiaozhuan have become the same component in Lishu.

The Beautiful and Elegant *Yiying Stele* (Eastern Han Dynasty)

The Sturdy and Graceful *Shichen Stele* (Eastern Han Dynasty)

The Vigorous and Lively *Ode to Xixia* (Eastern Han Dynasty)

" 心 xin (heart)" in Xiaozhuan changed to " 氵 ", " 扌 " and " 忄 " as the left components in Lishu characters. Many different strokes in Xiaozhuan characters changed to the same component in Han Li characters. For example, the claw and tail in the Xiaozhuan character " 鸟 bird" , the tails in the two characters of " 燕 swallow" and " 鱼 fish" , and the leg and tail in the character " 马 horse" all changed to four dots in Han Li characters. The last pictographic lines of Xiaozhuan disappeared.

Elegant Styles of Han Li

Many Lishu characters have been preserved on bamboo and wood strips and stone steles, and the highest achievement of ancient Lishu is displayed on the stele inscriptions of the Eastern Han Dynasty (25–220 AD). There are a large number of stele inscriptions of Lishu of the Eastern Han Dynasty with various styles and a high level of sophistication. For example, the Stele of Sacrificial Vessels with its solemn but deeply attractive calligraphy style, the beautiful and elegant Yiying Stele, the sturdy and simple Zhangqian Stele, the unrestrained Ode to Shimen with various forms, and the vigorous and lively Ode to Xixia have always been regarded as the most excellent models for students of calligraphy to copy and follow. In 175 AD Cai Yong (133–192), a great scholar of the Eastern Han Dynasty, in collaboration with some others, wrote major Confucian classics in the Lishu style, such as Shi Jing (Classics of Poetry), Shang Shu, and the Analects of Confucius. They were carved on 46 stone steles by famous craftsmen, which were set up at the door of Luoyang Taixue (the Imperial College), i.e. the famous Xiping Shijing. It is said that at that time many intellectuals came to Luoyang to see and learn Shijing. Before the Imperial College, "every day there were more than 1,000 carriages" that blocked the road. Xiping Shijing is the earliest official Confucian classic in China, and the Lishu characters inscribed on it have become the standard representative works of Han Li and are regarded as its masterpieces. Only a few relics of the Xiping Shijing have survived to the present day.

Standard Calligraphy Style – Kaishu

Kaishu (regular script), also known as "Zhenshu" (meaning real script) or "Zhengshu" (meaning regular script), received its name because it can serve as an example (Kaimo in Chinese) for learning calligraphy. Kaishu appeared at the end of the Eastern Han Dynasty (25–220) and evolved from Lishu (Han Li). In the Sui (581–618) and Tang (618–907) Dynasties it became considerably more mature. Kaishu is easier to write than Lishu and easier to read than Caoshu (cursive hand), so even up to the present day it is still popular and has become a standard calligraphy style with the widest and longest usage.

Lishu	春江花月夜
Kaishu	春江花月夜

The Comparison between the Strokes of Lishu and Kaishu. The strokes of Kaishu have no wave or tendency to rise at their endings like Lishu.

Upright and Foursquare Han Characters

It is said that in the Three Kingdoms (220–280) a minister of Wei State, Zhong You, wrote the earliest Kaishu. He changed the wave-like strokes of Lishu to horizontal and vertical lines, and the endings of horizontal, left-falling and right-falling strokes did not rise upward. There appeared the hook stroke, and the form became upright and foursquare. These changes made the writing of characters easier and were actually a kind of simplification. Kaishu characters have foursquare forms, symmetrical and precise structures, and generous and beautiful strokes, and the square characters are completely closed. By comparison, it is obvious to see that Kaishu and Lishu are basically the same as regards structure and form and are only different in respect of their strokes. The strokes of Kaishu are straight and have no wave or tendency to rise at their endings like Lishu.

Eight Strokes of Character " 永 yong"

In ancient times the eight strokes of the character " 永 " for learning

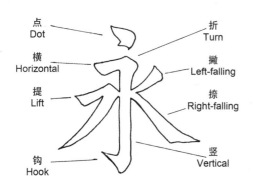

点 Dot
横 Horizontal
提 Lift
钩 Hook
折 Turn
撇 Left-falling
捺 Right-falling
竖 Vertical

Schematic Diagram of Eight Strokes of Character "永 yong"

Kaishu clearly demonstrated the eight basic strokes of Kaishu: dot, horizontal, vertical, left-falling, right-falling, turn, lift and hook strokes. In order to master the basic strokes of Kaishu, a person ought to write the character "永" repeatedly and this good way of practicing Kaishu was adopted by ancient people.

Yan Tendon and Liu Bone

In ancient times, many great calligraphers who practised Kaishu exhibited different styles in their strokes. For example, in the Tang Dynasty (618–907) the strokes of Yan Zhenqing's (709–785) characters are full and sturdy, whereas the strokes of Liu Gongquan's (778–865) characters are thin and rigid. Hence the phrase "Yan tendon and Liu bone" or "Yan fat and Liu thin" used to describe the different Kaishu styles of these two scholars. Take another example. The Kaishu characters of Ouyang Xun (557–641) in the Tang Dynasty are round, fluent, square and forceful, and the Kaishu characters of Zhao Mengfu (1254–1322) in the Yuan Dynasty (1206–1368) are round and fluent. People still refer to Yan Zhenqing, Liu Gongquan, Ouyang Xun and Zhao Mengfu as the four great ancient Kaishu calligraphers in China.

Kaishu of Yan Zhenqing

Kaishu of Liu Gongquan

Kaishu of Ouyang Xun

Kaishu of Zhao Mengfu

Most Common Character Styles

The Han characters used today are in the style of printed and handwritten Kaishu. Since the invention of printing in the Song Dynasty (960–1279) Kaishu has always been the major style for printing books, magazines and newspapers (Kaishu and variants of Kaishu, i.e. Songti or Song-Dynasty style, Fangsongti – imitation of Song-dynasty style, and Heiti – boldface style). These print-style characters are divided into different grades according to size to satisfy the demands of printing. In the printing style, the strokes are horizontal or vertical, clear and beautiful, the structure is ordered and symmetric, and these characters are most favored by the reading public.

Kaishu represents a style at the last stage of its evolution. Since the formation of Kaishu there has been, except for a degree of structural simplification, no major change.

A Lively and Vigorous Cursive Hand

The cursive hand is the simplified and continuous writing of Lishu characters. It breaks the square forms of Han characters. The lines are fluttering, the strokes are connected together and the resulting characters are lively and vigorous. It is hard to read characters thus written. Not exactly practical, but of great aesthetic quality. The cursive hand is divided into Zhangcao, Jincao and Kuangcao. Zhaocao is the cursive hand of initial stage, while Jincao is evolved from Zhaocao. As the latest and maturest kind of cursive hand, Kuacao is quite unique. The written Kuangcao characters are very lively and vigorous, and such

Cursive Hand *Four Ancient Poems* of Zhang Xu

works have great artistic value and are generally admired. In China there are many masters of cursive-hand calligraphy, such as Zhang Xu (675–750), a great calligrapher of the Tang Dynasty (618–907). His Kuangcao works are free, bold and unrestrained and full of motion and enthusiasm. People very much admire Zhang Xu's cursive-hand works and refer to him as "the master of cursive handwriting".

Fluent and Practical Running Hand

Running hand is the result of writing Kaishu rapidly. The characters thus formed are neither as ordered as Kaishu nor as elegant as cursive writing. It is a style somewhere between the regular script and cursive hand and is easy to recognize. If we can say that Kaishu seems like "sitting" and cursive hand resembles "flying", then running hand seems like "walking" . Running hand is extremely practical and the characters written by people on a day-to-day basis are usually of this sort. In ancient China, however, there were many great calligraphers of running hand, such as Wang Xizhi (303–361) of the Eastern Jin Dynasty (317–420). Wang Xizhi was an outstandingly great calligrapher in ancient China and expressed his considerable talent in Kaishu, running hand and cursive hand. People called him "the master of calligraphy". The *Lan Ting Xu*, written by Wang Xizhi in running hand style, has beautifully formed characters and fluent strokes and the work is honored as being the "No.1 running-hand work all the world".

永和九年歲在癸丑暮春之初會
于會稽山陰之蘭亭修禊事
也羣賢畢至少長咸集此地
有崇山峻領茂林修竹又有清流激
湍暎帶左右引以為流觴曲水
列坐其次雖無絲竹管弦之
盛一觴一詠亦足以暢敘幽情
是日也天朗氣清惠風和暢仰
觀宇宙之大俯察品類之盛
所以遊目騁懷足以極視聽之
娛信可樂也夫人之相與俯仰
一世或取諸懷抱悟言一室之內

Xingshu *Lan Ting Xu* of Wang Xizhi (Copy of Original of Tang Dynasty)

Mainstream in the Development of Han Characters

If a character has two or more forms, the one with more strokes is called a complex character while the one with fewer strokes is called a simplified character. Since ancient times, complex and simplified characters have coexisted, and the process of simplification has continued. Simplification is the mainstream of the development of Han characters.

Simplification of Han Characters in History

For hundreds, even thousands, of years Han characters have always faced a problem: they are difficult to learn, difficult to write and difficult to memorize. In order to try and change this situation, people have never stopped trying to simplify the characters. In the history of the development of Han characters such simplification has been continuous. Ancient China had witnessed a great simplification of Han characters several times, such as the evolution from Dazhuan to Xiaozhuan and from Xiaozhuan to Lishu. The ordinary folk people had further created simplified characters by means of simpler strokes, which was called "characters of nonstandard forms" at that time. Maybe you cannot believe that most of the current simplified characters are what we

The Simplification of Character " 车 (车)". All the characters in the pictures are ancient character" 车 "while the primary picture shows the wooden chariot of Shang Dynasty unearthed in Yin's ruins in Anyang, Henan.

云	网	胡	电	从	众	虫	来	杯
寿	与	发	声	怜	亲	旧	当	党
亚	坏	风	总	灯	战	机	虽	担
务	边	实	尔	无	气	礼	个	处
宝	时	节	声	梦	厅	灵	远	劝

Ancient simplified characters. They are created by ancient people and popularly used among ancient folk, which have been the standard simplified characters for people's daily use.

Prosperous Scene in Suzhou (Qing Dynasty). The plaques in the picture contain many simplified characters. The ancient folk people had further created simplified characters, which was called "characters of nonstandard forms" at that time.

call "nonstandard forms". Some people think that they were first painted by philologists in very old book-lined studies, but this is simply not true.

Simplification of Han Characters Today

Since the foundation of the People's Republic of China in 1949, the Chinese Government has adopted the simplification of Han characters as part of a major program of standardization of characters. It principally covers two aspects: the reduction of strokes and a reduction in the number

杯——盃	略——畧	启——啟
哲——喆	岳——嶽	峰——峯
考——攷	群——羣	同——仝
叫——呌	采——採	布——佈
决——決	辉——煇	减——減
迹——蹟、跡		
回——囘、囬、廻		

Examples of Reduction in the Number of Characters. The reduction in the number of characters mainly refers to abolishing variant Chinese characters. In the picture, the former character of each group is the standard character while the latter is abolished variant Chinese character.

of characters. The current simplified characters used on Chinese mainland were fixed on the basis of an ongoing study that has been conducted by the Chinese Government since 1956. In 1964 China issued the General Table of Simplified Characters, and in 1986 it further issued an updated version. A total of 2,263 complex characters have been replaced by 2,235 simplified characters, representing one-third of the total current characters. After simplification, the strokes of Han characters were reduced by nearly 50 percent, and the speed at which they can be written has been correspondingly increased.

Today, any character not complying with the General Table of Simplified Characters is not a standard character, such as the complex characters of " 學 (学) xue" and " 習 (习) xi" which have had simplified forms; variant Chinese characters which have been abolished, such as

" 盃 (杯) bei" , " 採 (采) cai" and so on. Those simplified characters not included in the General Table or created by someone himself, such as " 亍 (街)" , " 辺 (道)" , cannot be used. It is appropriate to remark here that complex characters are not standard characters, nor are they incorrect. They are still used in the compilation of ancient books, in the study of Chinese and in works of calligraphy. In 2013, the government of China issued General Standard Chinese Characters Table, in which a total of 8,105 general standard Chinese characters have been identified.

Well-formed characters have definite meanings and are able to be written fast. For instance, complex character " 龜 (gui)" does depicts what a tortoise is like, but difficult to be written due to quite some strokes, it's simplified one " 龟 (gui)" also shows the look of a tortoise, only 7 strokes contribute to a convenience and efficiency in writing. Take " 憂 鬱 (you yu)" as another example, also with many strokes, would be easier to be written when it is simplified into " 忧郁 (you yu)" . Simplified characters are convenient for people to write, and match with the development direction of characters. Now, the usage of simplified characters has become wider and wider. Both the Chinese mainland and the international community have adopted them. The Chinese versions of UN documents make use of simplified characters.

In history, ancient Chinese had, on many occasions, witnessed grand schemes of simplification. Now, the current simplified characters are another great simplification, which is actually an overall summary and standardization for the long-standing folk simplified characters.

FORMATION OF HAN CHARACTERS

The study of the formation of Han characters is the study of the ways to creat Han characters.

Han characters originated from drawings. The earliest Han characters were paintings of the things that people saw in front of them. The total number of Han characters is about 50,000 to 60,000. It is, of course, quite impossible to form so many characters by way of drawing. In fact, the clever ancient Chinese people very early figured out how to form Han characters by four methods, i.e. pictograph, indication, associative compounds, and phonograms.

Ancient Formation of "Six Categories"

Shuowen Jiezi (Origin of Chinese Characters), a famous work in the study of ancient characters, was written during the Eastern Han Dynasty (25–220), which is one of the oldest dictionaries in the world.

Xu Shen wrote *Shuowen Jiezi*

In the Western Han Dynasty (206 BC–25AD), Emperor Han Wudi (140–87 BC on the throne) adopted the thoughts of Confucius (551–479 BC) and Mengzi (372–289 BC) as the basis of his feudalist domination philosophy and emphasized Confucian thought in order to strengthen the unification of the state. Therefore, the study of Confucian classics became popular. In order to study Confucian thought, Emperor Han Wudi established "Taixue (Imperial College established in the capital in ancient times)" in Chang'an (present-day Xi'an, Shaanxi) and also set up the very special "five-classics court academicians" (equivalent to modern-day professors) to teach the five Confucian classics, namely Classic of Poetry, Book of Documents, Book of Rites, Classic of Changes and Spring and Autumn Annals. At that time, the classics were written in the popular Lishu style which belongs to the school of "modern characters", so these classics were called "modern-character classics". At the end of the reign of Emperor Han Wudi, some classics written in Dazhuan, i.e. "ancient characters", were

Figure of Xu Shen

found inside the walls of Confucius' old house, and these texts have become known as "ancient-character classics". The existence of two different kinds of characters adversely affected people's understanding of the classics, so a contention arose between the school of modern-character classics and the school of ancient-character classics, and it lasted for at least 200 years. In order to explain more accurately the ancient-character and modern-character classics, Xu Shen (58–147)(who himself belonged to the ancient-character classics school) in the Eastern Han Dynasty (25–220) spent 22 years writing the *Shuowen Jiezi* (*Origin of Chinese Characters*) based on his analysis of the structures of ancient characters. In *Shuowen Jiezi*, Xu Shen used the formation of the "six categories" to analyze and summarize ancient Han characters, created the study method of integrating forms, pronunciations and meanings and made great contribution to China's paleography.

The Old House of Confucius. It is said that when Emperor Qinshihuang of the Qin Dynasty burnt Confucian books, the surviving relatives of the great Master hid many of his classics, written in Dazhuan characters, inside the walls of Confucius's house, such as the Analects of Confucius, Shang Shu, and Chun Qiu (The Spring and Autumn Annals). They were discovered during the reign of Emperor Wudi of the Western Han Dynasty. These Confucian texts written in Dazhuan characters are ancient-character classics.

Shuowen Jiezi (Origin of Chinese Characters)

Shuowen Jiezi consists of 15 volumes and within are collected 9,353 characters classified into 540 components. With Xiaozhuan as the major characters, Xu Shen analyzed the forms and structures of written Chinese and comprehensively explained the forms, pronunciations, and meanings of Xiaozhuan, so that this book became the first dictionary of ancient characters in China. With the explanation of the meanings of Xiaozhuan characters based on their forms, *Shuowen Jiezi* offers us a wonderful opportunity to learn the structures of Han characters and grasp their original meanings, and is still a very useful reference book on ancient writing. Xu Shen did not see any Jiaguwen characters, which influenced the reliability of his analysis regarding some characters in the book, but the basic contents are correct. The study method of integrating forms, pronunciations and meanings originated by Xu Shen, the indexing system he invented based on the components for Han characters, and the enormous amount of material about ancient characters which his book has preserved for us have made this volume one of the most precious treasures for the study of Han philology.

Formation of the "Six Categories"

In *Shuowen Jiezi*, Xu Shen discussed the formation of the "six categories" of Han characters, i.e. pictographic characters, indicative characters, associative compounds, phonograms, mutually explanatory characters, and phonetic loan characters (currently the former four kinds are regarded as the ways of creating characters). With the integration of these six categories, he analyzed the formation of 9,353 Han characters. Xu Shen analyzed and summarized the ancient characters by means of the "six-category" formulation, which remains a most significant contribution to the philology of ancient characters in China. Right up to the present day the "six

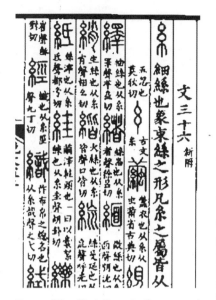

Copy of the First Page in Component Category of "丝 si" in *Shuowen Jiezi*. All the characters under the category of "丝 si" have the component of 纟, and the first listed 系 in the style of Xiaozhuan is the component.

categories" still play a role in analyzing the forms and structures of modern Han characters. Almost 50 percent of the current simplified characters we read and use today can be analyzed by the principle of the "six categories".

Components

    The system of components was established for ease of dictionary reference and was a great invention by Xu Shen. In *Shuowen Jiezi* (*Origin of Chinese Characters*) Xu Shen classified the 9,353 characters collected in the book into 540 categories. The characters within each category had the same component, and the first character in each category was the component. Therefore there were 540 components. A component represented a major "category", 540 components represented 540 categories, and each category included many things. The establishment of a component system not only offers convenience for looking up characters in a dictionary but also gives prominence to the function of expressing the meanings of Han characters. It is extremely useful when we want to learn and use Han characters. Regarding the major dictionaries in China, there are at present 214 components in *Ci Yuan* (*Origin of Vocabularies*), 200 in *Hanyu Dazidian* and *Hanyu Dacidian* (*Grand Chinese Dictionary*), 250 in *Ci Hai* (*The Sea of Vocabulary*), 189 in *Xinhua Zidian* (*Xinhua Dictionary*), and 201 in *Xiandai Hanyu Changyong Zibiao* (*Table of Common Characters in Modern Chinese Language*).

Formation Methods of Han Characters

The formation methods for Han characters were actually summarized after their appearance on the basis of the great number of ways in which they could be made. Han characters appeared before the study on formation of the "six categories" was raised, namely the formation method for Han characters. It is not the reverse.

Pictographic Characters

Pictographic characters use lines to directly represent things and look like drawings. There are relatively few in Han characters, but still serve as the basis for the characters themselves. Pictographic characters have a single form that cannot be divided into two or more characters, so they are also known as "independent characters".

Readable "Drawings"

Ancient Chinese people took themselves, along with animals and all the natural things around them as the models for drawing and thereby created some drawing-like pictographic characters. These characters as first created were all nouns. They not only indicated meanings but also contained pronunciation. For example, " ⊙ (日)" looks like the sun and is pronounced rì, " ⋀ (山)" looks like mountain peaks and is pronounced

Pictographic Characters in Jiaguwen. The pictographic characters in the famous cattle-bone inscriptions of the Shang Dynasty are very vivid.

shān, " 〔 (人)" looks like the profile of a person and is spoken rén, and " 〔 (鹿)" looks like a running small deer and is articulated as lù. They all have pronunciations and are characters instead of merely drawings.

Drawing out the Features of Things

The ancient pictographic characters are analogous to painting exactly because they represent the typical features of different things. For example, the round " 〇 (日 , sun)", bent " 〕 (月 , moon)", stable " 〰 (山 , mountain)", flowing " 〕 (水 , water)", standing " 〔 (人 , person)", big-head " 〇 (子 , boy)", posture of " 〇 (女 , girl)", horns of " 〇 (鹿 , deer)", the mane of " 〇 (马 , horse)", straight horns of " 〇 (牛 , ox)", curved horns of " 〇 (羊 , sheep)", long trunk of " 〇 (象 , elephant)", rolled-up tail of " 〇 (犬 , dog)", fat body and downward-pointing tail of " 〇 (猪 , pig)", and the teeth and long, thin tail of " 〇 (鼠 , mouse)" were all painted exactly, vividly, and in a lively way, with a strong abstract interest. They seem like exquisite artworks and we never tire of looking at them, even if it's for the hundredth time. The simplification of modern Han characters also adopted formation methods of pictographic characters, while some simplified characters are closer to pictographic charaters than complex characters.

Line Art of Han Characters

Han characters are a kind of line art. Those from the time of Jiaguwen (inscriptions on animal bones or tortoise shell) to the present day are all structures and forms of lines. Line is both the foundation and the most important feature of Chinese sculptural art, as well as a traditional aesthetic representation of the Chinese spirit. The profound mystery of traditional Chinese painting and calligraphy is in its lines. To understand these lines is to understand Chinese art. It is worth mentioning in this context that some great western painters, such as Pablo Picasso, Henri Matisse and Paul Gauguin, drew inspiration from the lines of oriental art and created some of their finest works accordingly.

Abstract Line Art

Being all based on ancient pictographic characters, the pictographic Han characters are different from those of other nationalities. They have concise lines and the painted things are simultaneously both real and not real. They are at the same time abstract and also representative of the typical features of things. These ancient pictographic characters are all vivid and lively. Their abstract interest and artistic qualities put one in mind of the works of Picasso, a great Spanish painter.

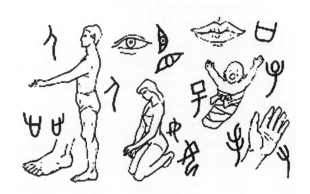

The pictographic characters were created on the basis of daily human experience and with distinctive features.

Those pictographic characters which describe animals represent the typical features of the animals in question.

Pictographic Interest

Ancient Han characters' forms have strong pictographic interest, and even the Kaishu characters of today, although not pictographic, can also give people the same impression as they might get from a painting. For example, the Kaishu character " 笑 xiao (smile)" looks just like a real smile, and a reader feels a corresponding happiness when he sees it. The character

" 喜 xi (happy)" also looks like the appearance of an opened-mouth smile and imparts a joyful feeling. The character " 哭 ku (cry)" looks like a loudly-crying person and cannot but help feeling sad also. The character " 甩 shuai (cast)" one sees on the doors of shops indicating "on sale" looks like a hand throwing things out onto the street outside and means that the store-keeper wants to give away money. In the smoke of the marketplace the character " 串 chuan (kebab)" really resembles a great big mutton kebab and therefore attracts customers. Even people who do not know Chinese characters can understand " 凸 tu (protruding)" and " 凹 ao (concave)". The character " 勺 sháo (spoon)" has a handle and contains food and also provokes an understanding smile. In addition, some phrases make use of forms of characters to describe the features of things, such as 国字脸 (a face

The Famous Painting by Picasso, Guernica. Picasso made use of distorted forms and symbolic method to compose a scene fully expressive of human misery, revealing the atrocity of the German fascists when their air force bombed the small Spanish town of Guernica in 1937. The painting is full of strong inspiration.

This Writer's Pen Painting, Pictographic Han Characters. This painting shows in a very artistic manner the pictographic quality of some ancient Han characters such as " 日 ri (sun), 月 yue (moon), 明 ming (bright), 女 nv (girl), 目 mu (eye), 泪 lei (tear), 木 mu (tree), 鸟 niao (bird), 集 ji (perch), 牛 niu (ox), 羊 yang (sheep), 牢 lao (pen), 犬 quan (dog), 京 jing (artificial mound), 火 huo (fire), 止 zhi (foot), 手 shou (hand) and 草 cao (grass)".

with the form like the character " 国 "), 八字胡 (moustache with the form like character "八"), 八字腿 (graphically representing a pair of legs by means of " 八 "), and 丁字尺 (a ruler in the form like the character " 丁 "). They are all interesting.

Pictographic characters should reveal the forms of all things, but this is, of course, quite impossible, for any language must include many abstract concepts, so there are not so many pictographic characters in Chinese. Among the 9,353 characters in *Shuowen Jiezi*, there are only about 300 pictographic characters. But they are basis of the formation of Han characters.

Indicative Characters

Indicative characters use symbolic signs or add indicative signs to pictographic characters to indicate meaning. They are also "independent characters". The numeric characters such as " 一 yi (one)", " 二 er (two)" and " 三 san (three)" are typical indicative characters with symbolic signs. " 木 (本)ben (root)", " 刀 (刃)ren (blade)", and " 甘 (甘)gan (sweet)" are all indicative characters with indicative signs added to the pictographic characters. For example, add a cross line at the bottom of the pictographic character " 木 mu (tree)" and you have the root (本) of the tree. Add a dot at the edge of the pictographic character " 刀 dao (knife)" and this indicates the blade " 刃 " of a knife. Add a cross line inside the pictographic character " 口 kou (mouth)" and now you have something with a sweet taste, for " 甘 gan (sweet)" means sweet. Other characters such as " 二 (上)shang (up)", " 下 (下) xia (down)", " 末 (末)mo (end)", " 亦 (亦)yi (also)", and " 血 (血)xue (blood)" are all common indicative characters with

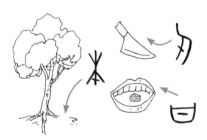

The Formation of Indicative Characters " 本 ben (root)", " 刃 ren (blade)", and " 甘 gan (sweet)"

correspondingly indicative signs. Indicative characters, it is true, can express some simple abstract concepts, but it is very hard for them to express complex concepts, so there are very few indicative characters among those of the Han, and only about 100 in the *Shuowen Jiezi*.

Associative-Compounds Characters

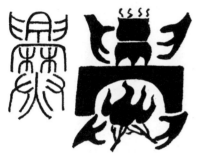

The Formation of Associative-Compounds Character "爨 cuan (cook)". The character " 爨 cuan (cook)" is actually a drawing representing the act of cooking in ancient times. On the left is the Xiaozhuan character of " 爨 cuan (cook)". If you look very carefully, you will see that it is extremely pictographic.

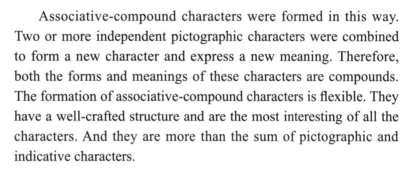

Associative-compound characters were formed in this way. Two or more independent pictographic characters were combined to form a new character and express a new meaning. Therefore, both the forms and meanings of these characters are compounds. The formation of associative-compound characters is flexible. They have a well-crafted structure and are the most interesting of all the characters. And they are more than the sum of pictographic and indicative characters.

Let's take a look at the associative-compound character " 爨 cuàn (cook)". The character " 爨 " means cook and it is composed of many pictographic characters with many strokes. As to its Xiaozhuan character form, the upper part is a " 甑 zeng (vessel for steaming food)" with double handles on a kitchen range, and the lower part is two hands that are putting burning logs into a kitchen range. The whole character describes the situation of cooking. A person not knowing this character can still understand its meaning. It means fire and cooking. This character is rarely used today and it has no simplified form. It can be said to be the most complex and interesting associative-compound character.

Associative-compound characters are divided into same- and different-compound characters. And there are more different-compound characters.

Same-Compound
Characters Composed of
Character " 人 ren (person)"

Same-Compound Characters. Each same-compound character is composed of several identical characters. For example, " 林 (林) lin (woods) "is composed of two " 木 mu (tree)" and means a woods which is made up of many trees. " 森 (森) sen (forest)" is composed of three " 木 mu (tree)" and means a forest, which is composed of many many trees. The meanings of " 林 " and " 森 " are the result of the compounds of two and three repeated characters, and the two characters are same-compound characters. Other common characters such as " 北 bei (north)", " 从 cong (follow)", " 炎 yan (very hot)", " 磊 lei (heap of stones)", " 淼 miao (expanse of water)", and " 晶 jing (brilliant)" are all same-compound characters. There are less same-compound characters.

Different-Compound Characters. Each different-compound character is composed of several different characters. For example, " 休 (休) xiu (have a rest)" is composed of two different characters, i.e. " 人 ren (a person)" and " 木 mu (tree)". A person relaxing against a tree means taking a rest. " 明 (明) ming (bright)" is composed of two shining characters, i.e. " 日 ri (sun)" and " 月 yue (moon)" and means an abundance of light. The combined meaning of the two characters is the result of the compounds of the meanings of each, and these are different-compound characters. Some words consisting of different-compound characters are also very interesting. For example, " 忐忑 (tǎn tè, means mentally disturbed)" composed by two different-compound characters, implies the heart bounces up and down, making someone be uneasy. As the saying goes, "(His heart seems to him) like a well in which seven buckets are drawn up and eight dropped down— an unsettled state of mind". A large part of Han characters are different-compound characters.

Some interesting different-compound characters (decoded from ancient Jiaguwen characters):

见 (jian, see)

" 见 (見)" is composed of " 目 mu (eye)" and " 人 ren (person)" . It utilized the depiction of a very big eye to indicate the act of seeing something, i.e., something shining before one's eye. " 见 jian (see) " is different from " 看 kan (look)" , the former represents the result and the latter represents the action. The eye was given prominence to express the result, and it is very artful!

祭 (ji, offer sacrifice)

It is composed of " 示 (sacrificial altar)", " (手 , hand)" and " (肉 , meat)".A hand is shown placing a piece of meat on a sacrificial altar and offering it to the gods or ancestors as part of an act of worship. The common words include " 祭祀 ji si (sacrifice)" , " 拜祭 bai ji (worship and sacrifice)", " 祭奠 ji dian (to hold a memorial ceremony for)" , and " 公祭 gong ji (a public memorial service)".

盥 (guan, to wash one's hands)

It is a drawing composed of " 手 (hands)" , " 水 (water)" , and " 皿 (utensil)": there is water between the pair of hands and there is also a basin containing water at the bottom " 盥 " means to wash one's hands and face. On the door of some public toilets in China, you will see a plaque upon which is " 盥洗 室 guan xi shi" , with " 洗 " meaning "wash" and " 室 " meaning " room".

涉 (she, wade)

Think of a person striding forward, one foot at a time, and you can appreciate the ancient character of " 步 bu (step)" . The ancient character of " 涉 she (wade)" shows a river running between two feet, and this is the representation of wading across a river. The character " 涉 " means to cross a river on foot.

 灾 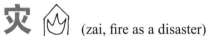 (zai, fire as a disaster)

Jiaguwen character " 灾 " is composed of " 宀 " and " 火 " . We can quite clearly see that a house is on fire. The modern simplified character has adopted the ancient. Besides the "fire disaster", the character can also be used to express other catastrophes, such as 水灾 shui zai (flood), 旱灾 han zai (drought), 风灾 feng zai (hurricanes) and 虫灾 chong zai (plagues of insects).

 进   (jin, advance)

" 进 (進)" is an excellent associative-compound character and reflects the ancient people's strong visual awareness of things. In Jiaguwen, the character " 进 " has a bird (the character " 隹 ") uppermost and a foot (the character " 止 ") beneath, indicating that a bird is walking or hopping forward on the ground. A bird can only go forward and cannot walk backwards, so this character means advance. Later " 止 " became " 辶 " , and this is the complex character " 進 " . Now, this character " 進 " has been simplified to " 进 " and has become a pictophonetic character.

 牧 (mu, herd)

" 牧 " means a herd of livestock. The ancient character " 牧 " is very interesting: an ox is in the forefront, and behind we can discern a hand driving the ox with a stick or branch. It is an interesting drawing about herding. And those words which include " 牧 " also have the same meaning, such as " 放牧 fang mu (herd)" , " 游牧 you mu (nomadism)" , " 牧羊 mu yang (shepherd)" , " 牧马 mu ma (the corralling of horses)" , and " 畜牧业 xu mu ye (livestock raising)" .

 # 逐  (zhu, chase)

" 逐 " means chase. In ancient times it had a very artistic formation: a wild boar (the character " 豕 ") is running, and is being followed by the foot (the character " 止 ") of a person, indicating that a hunter is chasing a wild boar. Later the character " 止 " changed to the form component " 辶 " indicating walk.

 # 津 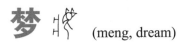 (jin, ferry)

The character " 津 " means ferry. In Jiaguwen, the character is actually a sketch of a ferry: a boatman is standing at the back of a boat, punting the vessel powerfully with a pole in his hands, and crossing a river. Later, the character dropped the " 船 (舟) (boat)" , and simply adopted a combination of " 河 水 (氵) (river)" and " 竿 (聿) (pole)" . Yet the meaning of the character is still very clear.

 # 梦 (meng, dream)

In Jiaguwen, " 梦 (夢)" depicted a man lying on a bed and having a dream: he is opening his eyes very widely, and raising his eyebrows, just as though he "is seeing" something in his sleep. Later this character omitted the " 床 (bed) " , added the " 夕 " indicating evening, and the eyebrows were altered. Now the simplified character is " 梦 " in which we can no longer see anything that we can really relate to the scene of someone having a dream.

寒 (han, cold)

It is composed of " 宀 (屋) (wu, house)" , " ⻗ (草) (cao, grass)" , " 人 (ren, person)" and " 冫 (冰) (bing, ice)" . A man is crouching in the grass inside his house, and there is ice on the ground, which gives the impression of cold. In modern Chinese, many phrases indicating extreme cold include the character " 寒 ", such as " 寒冷 han leng (very cold)" , " 寒风 han feng (cold wind)" , " 严 寒 yan han (chilliness)" , " 寒 假 han jia (winter vacation)", and " 天寒地冻 tian han di dong (the weather is cold and there is ice on the ground)" .

妻 (qi, wife)

A big hand grabs a woman's hair, the woman got back this way is the man's wife. This is a vivid statement related to the custom of "marriage by capture" in the ancient patriarchal clan society.

春  (chun, spring)

Jiaguwen character " 春 " is composed of " 日 ri (sun)" , " 木 mu (tree)" and " 屯 zhun (bud)" . The last " 屯 " , a phonetic character here, means the buds on the ground. The character " 春 " shows a vibrant spring scene, in which the sun shines and vegetation sprout. It is an associative compound, also a pictophonetic character.

焚 (fen, burn)

It has woods uppermost and raging fire beneath, means burning. Also, it lively reproduces the slash-and-burn cultivation (i.e., burning forests to cultivate the fields) in ancient times.

疑 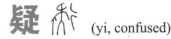 (yi, confused)

Jiaguwen character " 疑 " is very interesting. It depicts a man standing with a stick on the way, he looks left then right, and has no idea about which direction to go. It originally means confused and hesitated, later extended to doubt and suspicion.

旅  (lv, force)

In Jiaguwen, it is composed of a flag and two persons, just like the others gathering advance under the guidance of the fluttering military flag. It originally means army, later extended to travel. What interesting is that the ancient character " 旅 " is something like the scene in the modern society: a tour conductor guides visitors during the travel, holding a small flag.

Some different-compound characters form their meaning by the combining position of their separate parts. For example, " 小 xiao (small)" and " 大 da (big)" form the character " 尖 jian (sharp)", and " 上 shang (up)" and " 下 xia (down)" combine to produce " 卡 ka (get stuck)". Some different-compound characters express meaning directly by repeating the compounds. For example, " 小 土 xiaotu (small earth)" forms " 尘 chen (dust)", " 小 鸟 xiaoniao (small bird)" forms " 雀 que (sparrow)", " 不 正 buzheng (not central)" forms " 歪 wai (devious)", " 不好 buhao (not good)" forms " 孬 nao (bad)", " 不用 buyong (do not)" forms " 甭 beng (don't)", " 山石 shanshi (mountain stone)" forms " 岩 yan (rock)", " 山高 shangao (high mountain)" forms " 嵩 song (lofty)", " 大力 dali (great power)" forms " 夯 hang (ram)", and a development of " 手 shou (hand)" forms " 拜 bai (do obeisance)", whereas a separation of " 手 shou (hand)" forms " 掰 bai (break off)".

Among the simplified characters there are also many associative-compound characters produced by skillful combination, and they are worthy of our appreciation. For example, " 泪 lei (tear)" actually looks like an eye with a running tear, and " 笔 bi (pen)" is a brush-pen, with a bamboo stem and, at its tip, bristles. Other simplified characters, such as " 灶 zao (kitchen range)", " 双 shuang (double)", " 对 dui (answer)", " 尘 chen (dust)", " 体 ti (body)", " 国 guo (state)", " 孙 sun (grandson)", " 宝 bao (treasure)", " 帘 lian (curtain)", " 阴 yin (shade)", "阳 yang (bright)", and " 盖 gai (cover)" are all new associative-compound characters combined with great skill (and some are ancient common forms).

When studying the associative-compound characters, we found that independent characters that constitute the associative-compound characters all have dropped their own pronunciations. Take " 休 xiu (rest)" for example, though it is composed of independent character " 人 ren (person)" and " 木 mu (wood)" , the pronunciation is xiū rather than rén or mù. In other words, the radical of associative-compound characters is generally no longer phonetic, but revcals the meaning of the original character.

In a word, the formation of associative-compound characters is able to best represent not just meaning but the entire wisdom of the Chinese people. In the Chinese class, foreign students always enjoy the moment that teacher explains the associative-compound characters.

Pictophonetic Characters

In fact, there are more characters that can not be created in a pictographic, indicative and ideographic way. As for " 妈 ma (mother)" , " 姑 gu (aunt)" , " 姐 jie (elder sister)" and " 妹 mei (younger sister)" , how is it possible to invent these characters that all represent a female only through a pictographic, indicative and ideographic way? With the help of pronunciation, this is no longer a problem. Based on "女 nv (female)" , "妈" ,

Form Component	Sound Component	Han Character
氵	胡 hú	湖 hú
氵	青 qīng	清 qīng
氵	州 zhōu	洲 zhōu
氵	肖 xiāo	消 xiāo
氵	气 qì	汽 qì
氵	农 nóng	浓 nóng
氵	林 lín	淋 lín
氵	干 gān	汗 hàn
氵	羊 yáng	洋 yáng

No.1 Way of Formation of Pictophonetic Characters: Form Component + Sound Component

Sound Component	Form Component	Han Character
包 bāo	扌	抱 bào
包 bāo	月	胞 bāo
包 bāo	饣	饱 bǎo
包 bāo	氵	泡 pào
包 bāo	足	跑 pǎo
包 bāo	衤	袍 páo
包 bāo	火	炮 pào
包 bāo	刂	刨 bào
包 bāo	艹	苞 bāo

No.2 Way of Formation of Pictophonetic Characters: Sound Component + Form Component

" 姑 " , " 姐 " and " 妹 " are formed when respectively combined with " 马 ma (horse)" , " 古 gu (ancient)" , " 且 qie (moreover)"and " 未 wei (have not)" . This way, expressing meaning and with pronunciation, is called the formation way of pictophonetic characters. In the example just mentioned, " 妈 ", " 姑 ", " 姐 "and " 妹 " are pictophonetic characters.

Therefore, a pictophonetic character is composed of a form-component indicating meaning and a sound-component indicating pronunciation, which is also known as "character of combination". In other categories of characters, the components only indicate meaning, not pronunciation. The pictophonetic characters broke new ground by not purely indicating meaning, and a great number of characters could be formed in this way, so this method became the major way of forming characters. Now more than 85 percent of the Han characters are pictophonetic characters.

Two Formation Methods of Pictophonetic Characters

(1) Mark Sounds on Drawings

Only a few characters could be formed by means of pictograph, indication and associative compounds, because it is difficult to depend only on the association of forms and meanings of characters. For example, it is difficult to form the character " 湖 hu (lake)" by using these three formation methods, but it is easy when one employs the formation way of pictophonetic characters. In this way, " 氵 " (水) (water) was used as the form component to indicate something of which water is a part, and a ready-made character " 胡 " was used as the sound component to indicate its pronunciation, hence the character " 湖 ". If the sound component is changed to other characters with different pronunciations, more characters related to water would be created, such as " 泳 yong

(swim), 淋 lin (pour), 源 yuan (source), 液 ye (liquid), 洋 yang (sea), 汗 han (sweat) and 酒 jiu (wine)." Obviously, this formation method makes full use of the distinctiveness of pronunciation.

(2) Match Sounds with Drawings

Using a character indicating pronunciation as the sound component and matching it with characters of various different meanings as the form components also form many pictophonetic characters with the same or similar pronunciation. For example, the character " 包 bāo" is a sound component, and many pictophonetic characters with the same or similar pronunciations can be formed from it, such as " 抱 bào (hold in one's arms)", " 跑 pǎo (run)", " 泡 pào(steep)" , " 炮 pào(cannon)" , and " 苞 bāo (bud)". The structures show clearly: " 抱 " needs hand, " 跑 " needs foot and " 泡 " needs water. Obviously, this formation method makes full use of the distinctiveness of meaning.

Structure of Pictophonetic Characters

There are six ways of combining the sound and form components for pictophonetic characters: form on the left and sound on the right, form right and sound left, form up and sound down, form down and sound up, form out and sound in, and form in and sound out. Of these, the first mentioned, in which we have form on the left and sound on the right, describes the most characters, although form up and sound down are also frequently used.

The formation of pictophonetic characters is still used in the simplification of Han characters today. Among these simplified Han characters there are many new pictophonetic characters with concise form, exact pronunciation and definite meaning. For example, " 拥 yong (embrace)", " 护 hu (protect)", " 担 dan (carry on a shoulder pole)", " 拦 lan (hold back)", " 栏 lan (railing)", " 战 zhan (battle)", " 惊 jing (be frightened)", " 响 xiang (echo)", " 吓 xia (scare)", " 虾 xia (shrimp)", " 态 tai (attitude)", " 亿 yi (a hundred million)", " 忆 yi (recall)" , " 艺 yi (plant)",

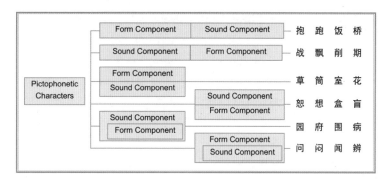

Six Ways of Combining the Sound and Form Components

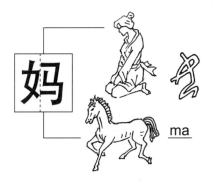

Formation of Character " 妈 ma (mother)". In the character " 妈 ma (mother)", the form component " 女 nv (female)" is a pictographic character, indicating that " 妈 妈 mama (mother)" is female, and the sound component " 马 ma (horse)" was loaned to indicate the pronunciation and was originally a pictographic character indicating horse.

" 让 rang (allow)" , " 坟 fen (tomb)" , " 疗 liao (cure)", and " 园 yuan (garden)" are all new pictophonetic characters that have been successfully simplified.

Promotion of Characters' Function of Indicating Meanings

Pictophonetic characters are a kind of advanced method of formation. This method was no longer the simple way of drawing, but went far beyond in its pure indication of meanings for forming characters and thus greatly increased the number of Han characters. Thus, pictophonetic characters became the principal part of Han characters. They have components indicating sounds, which imply that Han characters developed phonographically. But, basically speaking, Han characters are a system of ideographic characters, because in Han characters there are many pictographic, indicative, and associative-compound characters which directly use form to indicate meaning, such as " 人 ren (a person)" , " 本 ben (root)" and " 休 xiu (have a rest)" ; the pictophonetic characters have ideographic components which strongly indicate meaning, such as " 女 nv (female)" in the character " 妈 ma (mother)" ; and the sound components are actually graphic characters serving to indicate pronunciation. For example, in the pictophonetic character " 妈 ma (mother)" , " 马 ma (horse)" is a pictographic character. Furthermore, the frequent appearance of pictophonetic characters actually extended the use of graphic components and strengthened the characters' function of indicating meanings. Therefore, when the majority of Han characters became pictophonetic, their graphic quality became more prominent. Now we have found an answer to the question as to why there are such an enormous number of pictophonetic characters in the Han system, with a strong graphic function of form components, and this also gives us an important reason for why Han characters did not eventually become phonograms.

After a long period of evolution, the sound components we see today, consisting of many pictophonetic characters, do not represent the exact pronunciation, and it is worth bearing this in mind when we are either learning or using them.

Mutually Explanatory Characters and Phonetic Loan Characters

Mutually explanatory characters and phonetic loan characters are two kinds of usage of Han characters, which will be introduced briefly.

Mutually explanatory characters. Mutually explanatory characters are a kind of special formation within the ancient "six categories". It is generally believed that the name refers to a group of characters having the same components, same meanings and similar pronunciations. In the *Shuowen Jiezi*, the author used the two characters " 老 lao (old)" and " 考 kao (aged)" to illustrate this point. Both characters incorporate the component of " 老 lao (old)" and they have similar pronunciations and the same meaning, i.e. old. " 老 " is " 考 ", and vice versa. This is a good example of a mutually explanatory character. It was a way of using characters adopted by people long ago to explain one character by reference to another, but it was not a method of formation.

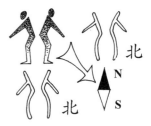

The character " 北 bei" expressing the meaning of "opposition" was loaned to indicate the direction of north (" 北 bei") and lost its original meaning. Therefore, " 北 bei" becomes phonetic loan character.

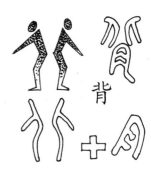

The character " 月 yue" was added to the character " 北 " to form the character " 背 bei" indicating the original meaning of "opposition". Therefore, " 背 bei" becomes pictophonetic character.

Phonetic loan characters. Phonetic loan characters are important in the development of Han characters. In linguistic terms, they use a ready-made character to record a newly produced homophonic character. In the Chinese language there is sometimes a word that does not have a character to represent it, and making a new character is very difficult. So what can we do? The simplest way is to borrow another character. For example, the associative-compound character " 北 bei" looks like two people standing back to back and originally means opposition and violation. Previously, no character simultaneously represented the meaning of direction and pronunciation of "běi". Due to the same pronunciation, the associative-compound character " 北 " was conveniently borrowed to represent the direction of north. When the character " 北 " became a phonetic loan character, would it express the meaning of opposition and violation or the loaned meaning of a direction? In order to differentiate between the meaning of the loaned character and its original meaning, it was necessary to create another character to express the original meaning. The form component " 月 (肉)(flesh)" , indicating the meaning of body, was added to the character " 北 " and the character " 背 " was created to express the original meaning. It is a way of adding a form component to solve the problem posed by phonetic loan characters, and is actually a formation of pictophonetic characters. Initially, most pictophonetic characters were formed in this way. It can be said that phonetic loan characters greatly pushed forward the formation and development of pictophonetic characters.

In ancient times there were many phonetic loan characters. And we now have many phonetic loan characters among our regularly used day to day characters and words, such as " 甲 jia (first), 乙 yi (second), 丙 bing (third), 丁 ding (fourth), 东 dong (east), 西 xi (west), 南 nan (south), 北 bei(north), 之 zhi (modal particle), 乎 hu (modal particle), 者 zhe (modal particle), 也 ye (modal particle), 而 er(while), 其 qi (its), 且 qie (and), 又 you (again), 咖啡 kafei (coffee), 纽约 niuyue (New York), 滴答 dida (tick), 哗啦 huala (clatter)."

Form and Structure of Modern Han Characters

In the eyes of Chinese people, the form and structure of Han characters are composed on several levels and there is a definite order in which they should be written, so it is really not at all difficult to write Han characters and they, the Chinese, are as adept at doing so as they are at eating with chopsticks. Modern Han characters are square characters composed of strokes, and the form and structure have three levels: stroke-component-character. Of these, the component is the core of the Han characters' form and structure.

Strokes and Orders of Strokes

Strokes

Strokes are the various dots and lines with which the Han characters are composed. In writing, a stroke begins as soon as the pen touches the paper and is completed when the pen is raised. There are eight basic strokes in Han characters: dots, horizontal strokes, vertical strokes, left-falling strokes, right-falling strokes, turning strokes, lifting strokes, and hook strokes. In addition, these basic strokes mostly have variants. For example, there are short and long vertical strokes, as well as vertical left-falling strokes, vertical turning strokes, vertical lifting strokes, vertical hook strokes, and vertical

BasicStroke	Name	Category	Example
、	Dot	、	主、下
		ノ	小、半
一	Horizontal stroke	一	十、下
		ˉ	士、未
丨	Vertical stroke	丨	丰、上
		ˌ	列、止
ノ	Left-falling stroke	ノ	乎、千
		ノ	风、片
\	Right-falling stroke	\	八、文
		⌣	之、这
㇕	Turning stroke	㇆	国、五
		L	区、母
㇀	Lifting stroke	㇀	打、习
		㇀	比、饭
し	Hook stroke	→|	买、军
		亅	小、可
		し	七、儿

Major Strokes of Han Characters and Its Variants

In the opening ceremony of 2008 Beijing Olympic Games, athletes from various countries walked into the stadium in the order of the number of stokes of the initial character of the country. The picture shows Delegation of Brazil who was the 38th team to enter the stadium.

turning hooks, and so forth. Han characters are composed of the basic strokes and the variants of these strokes. Modern Han characters are square in form. There are no round strokes in Han characters, and very few arcs. Only left-falling and right-falling strokes exhibit a small degree of curve, and the rest are basically straight lines. For example, the sun is round but the character " 日 ri (sun)" is square and composed of straight strokes. Of all the various strokes, horizontal and vertical strokes predominate, and being able to reproduce these is the basic requirement for writing Han characters. Each standard Han character has a fixed number, form and position for the strokes that cannot be randomly changed.

To make the form of Han characters balanced and beautiful, so say nothing of making the writing of them more convenient, their strokes will accommodate some changes in the form. For example, in the left component, when the last stroke is a horizontal stroke, it must change to a lifting stroke, such as the last strokes in the left components of the characters " 地 di (earth)" , " 现 xian (appear)", " 轮 lun (wheel)", and " 孩 hai (child)". In the left component, when the last stroke is a right-falling stroke, it must change to a dot such as the characters " 林 lin (woods)", " 灯 deng (lamp)" , " 利 li (sharp)", and " 剩 sheng (remnant)". When " 月 yue (moon)" is a component in the lower part of a character, the

first vertical left-falling stroke will change to a vertical stroke, such as the characters " 青 qing (blue)", " 前 qian (front)", " 能 neng (ability)", and " 谓 wei (tell)". We should pay attention to such changes in these strokes when writing Han characters.

Orders of Strokes

There is a specific order to the strokes when writing Han characters, and the rules are as follows: a horizontal stroke prior to a vertical one (十 shi, ten), a left-falling stroke prior to a right-falling one (人 ren, person), a upper stroke prior to a lower one (二 er, two), a left stroke prior to a right one (川 chuan, river), an outer part prior to an inner one (月 yue, moon), a central stroke prior to those on either side (小), and what we can best describe as entering before closing the door (国 guo, country). Writing Han characters according to the prescribed order does not just allow us to write them quickly and correctly, but also helps us to understand their structure. Not following the correct order is known as "inverted strokes", and in this case people cannot write Han characters quickly and correctly or properly grasp the structure of the characters. For example, when writing the character " 进 jin (enter)", the correct order is " 井 " prior to " 辶 ", and in this way the pen is able to be in just the right place for the next stroke.

Components

Generally speaking, we usually call components " 偏旁 piān páng" that are composed of strokes. Components are the basic parts from which Han characters are formed, bigger than strokes and smaller than characters. They are divided into character components (i.e. independent characters) and non-character components (variants of independent characters). In modern combined characters, each part is a component. For example, the character

" 好 hao(good)" is composed of " 女 nu (female)" and " 子 zi (baby)" which are both character components. The character " 谢 xie(thank)" is composed of a non-character component " 讠 " and character components " 身 shen (body)" and " 寸 cun(1/3 decimeter)". The three parts are all components. The components of " 衫 shan (sleeveless jacket)" are " 衤 " and " 彡 " which are both non-character components.

More than 1,000 years ago, the Suowen Jiezi (Origin of Chinese Characters) by Xu Shen set down the analysis of the Han characters' forms according to their components. Independent characters were the first things to be created in the formation of Han characters, and they were in turn used to produce the combined characters, so the independent characters are actually constituent parts of combined characters. By means of components, students of the Chinese language can connect the forms with the meanings and pronunciation of the characters. In addition, learning more components is extremely useful if you want to be able to look up characters in a dictionary. Now Han characters have been successfully put into computers by means of the "way of radicals", which was formed on the basis of the analysis of components.

Radicals

We have already said that Xu Shen invented "radicals". In his dictionary he classified characters with the same components into a category, and the first listed component character as the symbol is the radical, such as " 木 mu (tree)" and " 人 ren (person)". All the characters in the category with the radical of " 木 mu (tree)" have the component of " 木 " and all the characters in the category with the radical of " 人 " have the component of " 人 ". To put it simply, a radical can be thought of as the "head of a category". Generally speaking, radicals are components, but not all components are radicals. For example, the sound component of a pictophonetic character is a component, but it indicates the pronunciation and is not the radical. Most radicals are ideographic form components. It is more convenient to look up something in a dictionary with radicals.

A radical represents a large category, and in a dictionary there are usually more than 200 radicals representing the words within more than 200 categories. Each category includes many specific things, so these 200 odd radicals lead to tens of thousands of Han characters. For example, you can find the names of trees, various parts of trees and wood products under the radical of " 木 mu (tree)".

（一）部首目录

（部首右边的号码指检字表的页码）

一画		人(入) 18	厶 21	口 27	彐(彑彐)	夕 41	气 43
一 14		勹 18	又(ㄡ) 21	囗 28	35	车(車) 41	女 43
丨 15		勹(见刀)	廴 24	巾 29	尸 35	戈 41	片 43
丿 15		儿 18	廴 24	山 29	己(已) 36	比 41	斤 43
㇏ 15		几(几) 18	三画	彳 30	弓 36	止 41	爪(爫) 44
乙(一乛)		亠 18	工 21	彡 30	屮 36	攴 41	父 44
乚 15		冫 19	土 22	夂 31	女 36	攴 41	月(月) 45
二画		冖 19	士 22	夕 31	子(孑) 37	日 42	欠 45
二 15		辶(辶) 19	艹 22	夂 31	子(孑) 37	曰(冃) 42	风(風) 45
十 15		阝(邑) 20	卅(在下)	夊 31	马(馬) 38	水(氺) 42	殳 45
厂 16		阝(在左)	廾 24	食(飠) 31	幺 38	见(見) 42	文 45
匚 16		阝(在右)	大 24	彳(犭) 31	巛 38	牛(牛)	火 45
卜(⺊) 16		凵 21	尢 25	门(門) 31	四画	43	灬 46
刂 16		刀(勹) 21	寸 26	忄(心) 34	王 38	手 43	户 46
冂 16		力 21	弋 26	辶(辶) 34	韦(韋) 39	毛 43	衤(礻) 46
亻 16			小(⺌) 26	辶(辶辵) 35	木 39		
八(丷) 18					犬 41		

Index of Radicals in Hanyu Cidian (Chinese Dictionary)

Whole Characters

Whole characters are those in common usage, composed of several parts, and are a combination of form, pronunciation and meaning. Whole characters can be divided into single-part characters (independent characters) and multi-part characters (combined characters). In modern Han characters, there are only a few single-part characters representing less than 10 percent of the overall total. The other 90-plus percent are multi-part characters. Of these, the majority is composed of three parts and these account for over 40 percent of the total characters.

Single-part characters only have one part and are

人	木	水	土	山
心	目	女	子	鸟
羊	牛	犬	马	贝

Single-part characters are independent characters.

Structure of left and right	休 汗 跑 唱 楳
Structure of up and down	花 竿 架 爸 空
Encircled structure	园 围 问 闻 辨

Multi-part characters are combined characters.

independent. There are not many independent characters, but they are mostly ones that are in common usage and have a strong function of formation.

Multi-part characters are composed of two or more parts along with combined characters. They can be a combination of independent characters or else independent characters and components which have been changed from independent characters, such as " 明 ming (bright)" and " 森 sen (forest)" for the former category and " 抱 bao (hold in arms)" and " 笔 bi (pen)" for the latter. Combined characters are in the majority and there are principally three structures, i.e. left and right, up and down, and encircled, and most of them are composed of left and right parts. Combined characters are the majority of Han characters.

To learn the formation of Han characters is to learn their form and structure. They have the pictographic characters as the basis of their form and structure, and for this very important reason Han characters still exhibit strong ideographic quality. Although, as previously mentioned, Han characters are ideographic, nevertheless they indicate both meaning and pronunciation. With regard to formation and usage, the ideogram is their outstanding quality.

Causes of the Square Form of Han Characters

Among all the languages of all the nationalities of the world, the square form of Han characters enjoy unique charm.

It is not unusual for Han characters to select the square form. When the characters were first created, the ancient Chinese people deliberately selected the square form, and the ideogram of characters form and the independence of Chinese pronunciation decided that Han characters should be independent square forms.

Natural Selection in Aspect of Vision

When the characters were first created, the ancient Chinese had quite deliberately decided to select the square form, and numerous primitive rock paintings, symbols carved on pottery ware, and early characters are almost all square. The earliest character, the symbol of " 旦 " in the Dawenkou Culture, was obviously a rectangle; the earliest mature characters, i.e. the Jiaguwen, nearly all had irregular rectangular forms; Xiaozhuan characters, standardized by Emperor Qinshihuang of the Qin Dynasty (221–206 BC) were rectangular, which were relatively regular; after the change of Lishu, Han characters gradually became fixed on the square form, and the Kaishu characters we use today have a very regular square form. So we can definitely say that the square form is the fundamental formal feature of Han

Character " 来 lai (come)" in the " 米 " -shaped Pane. We can clearly see that the major strokes of the character " 来 " accord with the axis of the " 米 "-shaped pane, and this character appears very stable.

Balance of Structure in the " 米 "-shaped Pane: In the character " 扮 ban (to be dressed up as)" the left part is small while the right is big, but in the square form both left and right attain balance and this is what we refer to as "visual balance".

characters, and the evolution of Han characters was from an irregular to a regular square form.

The square form of Han characters was a result of a sort of natural selection based on visual appeal.

In respect of this visual appeal, the square form imparts a feeling of stability, for inside such a form there is an immediately apparent central point. It is the most stable place and the balancing point of force, and a character will lose this sense of balance if it deviates from it. This center point has a focal attractive force that operates on all the strokes inside the square form so that these strokes close in on the center and establish a balance of forces. The practice of writing Han characters inside the " 米 mi(rice)"-shaped panes is a good illustration of our point. The center point of a " 米 "-shaped pane is the intersecting point of four axes. The center point and the four axes are all in comparatively stable positions. It is a requirement that the major strokes of Han characters should at least approximately accord with these axes, in order that they achieve stability. For example, the major strokes of the character " 水 shui (water)" fundamentally accord with the axes, and the whole character is stable. If the character " 水 " is used as a component, the three strokes of "three-point 水 " are also directed towards the center point.

In addition, in order to obtain the desired visual balance, it is also necessary that the strokes on both sides or over and above the " 十 " axis should be basically symmetrical. For example, " 水 shui (water)" , " 木 mu (tree)" , " 林 lin (woods)", and " 扮 ban (to be dressed up as)" are symmetrical between the left and right, and " 显 xian (apparent)" , " 安 an (safety)" , " 胃 wei (stomach)" , and " 吕 lu " are equally symmetrical between top and bottom, and they all impart the visual impression of stability. Of course, in such symmetry, the left and right strokes, or those which go up and down, do not cover the completely same area, and the result is just a visual balance. When one looks at a square form, one might

easily gain the impression that the lower or right part is bigger, heavier, and more stable, so the Han characters with the most stable structure are usually smaller at the top and wider at the bottom, or smaller on the left-hand side and bigger on the right.

The Decisive Role of the Ideogram

Indication of Visual Image

Indication of meaning by the use of visual forms is the fundamental feature of Han characters. It can be said that the aim of Han characters is to transform expressed meaning into a visual and understandable form. For example, characters such as " 龙 long (dragon)" , " 休 xiu (rest)" , " 晶 jing (brilliant)" , " 花 hua (flower)"and " 国 guo (country)" all represent the spacial combination of strokes and components. Without a two-dimensional canvas of left and right and up and down, it would be impossible to form the great variety of Han characters that we actually have.

Alphabetic writing is different. It only indicates pronunciation but has no relation to meaning, the form is very simple, and there is no major issue regarding space, such as a, b, c, d, etc. In addition, the words composed from letters of the alphabet have a lineal arrangement, and idea of the square space is redundant. For example, the English word "dragon" is a lineal arrangement of six alphabetic letters, whereas the corresponding Han character " 龙 long" began as a drawing of a dragon. Later it became a combination of strokes, but they all required a square space. Therefore, the ideograms which developed into the Han characters needed a geometrical area within which they could achieve visual balance.

Independence of Syllables. Han characters are the basic structural units with which the Chinese language is recorded, and are the combination of pronunciation and meaning. Generally speaking, a character records

Square Character " 龍 (龙)long (dragon)". Since ancient times the drawing-like character " 龙 " has needed a square space. It is quite different from the English word dragon which has a linear structure.

one syllable, one syllable represents one morpheme, and the syllable corresponds to a character. For example, the character " 书 " represents the syllable "shū" , and this syllable in turn represents the morpheme of " 书 (book)" . It can be said that Han characters are very suitable for the practical situation of the Chinese language. For example, the word " 汉语 hanyu (Chinese)" consists of two syllables "hànyǔ" represented by two characters. One character records one syllable and one syllable is a character. The syllables of the Chinese language are independent and cannot be combined with other syllables. Also, the Han characters are independent and cannot be put together with, or be transformed into, other characters. So the independence of Chinese syllables was the deciding factor in Han characters corresponding to syllables and becoming independent square forms.

Unhindered by Numerous Dialects. Square characters are very suitable for the actual situation of Chinese language, which incorporates many dialects and a great number of homonyms. Han characters indicate their meanings by the use of forms, and these drawing-like forms give the reader a visual impression rather than an auditory sound, and therefore the misunderstandings caused by different dialects can be avoided. With different speech sounds, Chinese people in different parts of the country and of different ethnic groups can still understand the meanings of the characters, because what they see is square characters indicating meaning by virtue of form. The linear arrangement of alphabetic writing is not practicable in China. For example, a sentence of Mandarin (Putonghua) " 又有油, 又有肉 (there is both oil and meat)" would be pronounced as "you you you, you you you" according to Shandong dialect, and who can make sense of that? But the expressive way of six square characters can be understood everywhere across the country.

MYSTERY OF MODERN HAN CHARACTERS

Square Han characters are mysterious, and the pictographic elements hidden in their square forms are the great and wonderful mystery of these characters.

The Han characters are the graphic characters based on pictographic characters. Due to the evolution of strokes and their consequent simplification, modern Han characters are no longer pictographic characters, but the remnants of some ancient pictographic characters can still be discerned, i.e. the stroke symbols representing some meanings. The pictographic elements in the forms of Han characters are actually extremely helpful when we are studying or using Han characters.

Pictographic Elements in the Form of Modern Han Characters

By no means are the inanimate symbols, ancient pictographic characters actually vibrant, refined and textured ones. In modern Han characters, the remnants of some ancient pictographic characters can still be discerned, i.e., the stroke symbols representing some meanings: pictographic elements, which are sufficiently manifested in the independent and combined characters.

Pictographic Elements in Independent Characters

At first, the independent characters of Han characters were all pictographic. For example, the ancient form of the character " 日 ri (sun)" was a rounded sun, the " 山 shan (mountain)" was a literal painting of three peaks, the " 水 shui (water)" looked like a flowing river, " 人 ren (person)" was a profile of a person with arms outstretched, " 手 shou (hand)" was the shape of a hand with five fingers and " 马 ma (horse)" was the shape of a horse. In modern Han characters we no longer find such vivid drawings. Han character changed from pictographs to symbols, from drawings to strokes. However, the basic shapes of those drawings are still visible, while the character " 日 " has been changed from a round sun to a square sun and the three peaks of the " 山 " has been simplified into three vertical strokes. The remnants of some ancient pictographic characters are not only the stroke

The complex form of " 马 ma (horse)" was evolved from the ancient character which resembled a drawing. In the complex form " 馬 " the three horizontal strokes in the upper part are the long hair on a horses neck, the four dots in the lower part are its legs, the horizontal, vertical and turning strokes in the middle represent the head, body and tail.

symbols representing some meanings, but also the pictographic elements in the forms of Han characters.

In the Han system of writing, many independent characters have similar shapes, such as " 木 mu (tree)" and " 禾 he (ripened grain)". The difference between the two characters is only a horizontal left-falling stroke on the " 木 ", and this stroke is just the pictographic element which is used for differentiating the two characters. " 禾 " is grain with an ear, and the horizontal left-falling stroke is the ear itself.

Definite meaning and strong ideographic function mean that most independent characters have become radicals of combined characters. For example, " 日 " means both the sun and time, and the combined characters with " 日 " as their radical such as " 明 ming (bright)" , " 时 shi (time)" , " 晚 wan (evening)" , " 昨 zuo (yesterday)" , and " 旱 han (drought)" represent these meanings. The independent characters serving as radicals have fewer strokes and a strong function of formation, in addition to which they have fixed meanings and pronunciation, and in particular the pictographic elements in the characters' form are comparatively obvious. More than 90 percent of modern Han characters are composed of such radicals. In order to learn and use Han characters correctly, we should thoroughly know such independent characters serving as radicals, then we will soon be able to learn a large group of these characters.

Apparently, independent characters serving as radicals basically became the "components" in dictionaries. To get familiar to the independent characters serving as radicals in common use, the "index of radicals" of Chinese dictionary and thesaurus, in which important and frequently used independent are covered.

Independent Characters	Ancient Character Forms	Drawings of Characters' Origin	Analysis of Pictographic Elements
日			The rounded line of the ancient character of "日ri (sun)" gradually became the strokes of "口kou(mouth)" in the modern character, and the horizontal stroke in "日" was originally a dot in a circle.
山			The three vertical strokes were originally three peaks in the ancient character of "山shan (mountain)".
木			The vertical stroke was the trunk of the ancient character "木mu (tree)", the horizontal stroke was the branch, and the left-falling and right-falling strokes were the roots.
禾			"禾he (plant)" indicates plant, and the left-falling stroke is the ear of the plant.
女			The first and second strokes represent crossed arms and the horizontal stroke is the body.
母			The frame of the character is the variant of the ancient character "女nv (female)", the horizontal stroke in the middle is the body and the two dots inside represent her breasts.
子			The horizontal turning stroke in the upper part is the exaggerated head of the ancient character"子zi(child)",the vertical hook stroke indicates the body and one leg and the horizontal stroke represents the arms.

Independent Characters	Ancient Character Forms	Drawings of Characters' Origin	Analysis of Pictographic Elements
手			The left-falling stroke and two horizontal strokes indicate five fingers.
鱼 (魚)			(A complex character) The upper part is the fish's head, "田 tian(field)" is the fish's body, and the four dots are its tail.
马 (馬)			(A complex character) The three horizontal strokes above are the long mane on the horse's neck, the four dots below are its legs, and the horizontal, vertical and turning strokes in the middle represent the head, body and tail of the horse.
鼠			"臼 jiu(mortar)" is a mouse. It has the protruding teeth of a mouse, the strokes in the lower right part indicate the mouse's feet, and the last long stroke indicates the mouse's body and tail.
象			The stroke "⺈" is the trunk of an elephant, "⼞" is the elephant's head, the stroke in the lower middle part is the body, the stroke on the left is the leg, and the last stroke, the right-falling stroke, is the tail.
龙 (龍)			(A complex character) The left part is the dragon's head, "立 li(stand)" is the dragon's horns, "月 yue(month)" is an open mouth with sharp teeth, and the right bent stroke is the body and tail of the dragon.
车 (車)			(A complex character) The vertical stroke is the vehicle axle, the "田 tian(field)" in the middle is the wheels, and the two horizontal strokes above and below are the peg locking up the vehicle.
衣			The horizontal, left-falling and right-falling strokes compose two sleeves, and the vertical hook and short left-falling strokes are the lower hem of the clothes.

Pictographic Elements in Combined Characters

A combined character has several parts, such as " 明 ming (bright)", " 妈 ma (mother)" , " 河 he (river)" , " 把 ba (hold)" , and " 花 hua (flower)". Combined characters are, as we can quite plainly see, associative-compounds and pictophonetic characters. The pictographic elements of the combined characters are shown on the ideographic components, i.e. the form components, such as " 日 ri (sun)" and " 月 yue (moon)" in the associative-compound character " 明 " and " 女 nv (female)" in the pictophonetic character " 妈 " . The characters serving as form components are radicals. According to statistical evidence, among the 2,270 combined characters in the 2,500 common Han characters, 70 percent of the form components still function in the role of distinguishing the meanings.

Category Meanings of Form Components. It is important to grasp the category meanings of form components before one can get a true understanding of these form components, i.e. the basic meaning of a category which contains things with common qualities and features. For example, the form component " 氵 " represents such things as running "water" and "liquid" , and "water" and "liquid" are the category meanings of " 氵 " . Once we understand this, we will quite easily learn the combined characters related to "water" and "liquid" , such as " 河 he (river)" , " 油 you (oil)" , " 汗 han (sweat)" , " 流 liu (flow)", " 澡 zao (bath)" , and " 泡 pao (bubble)" . Let us take another example. The form component " 疒 " was, in the ancient characters, a representation of a sweating person lying on a bed, implying that this person was sick. It is hard to see such a vivid scence from the modern character " 病 ", but we can notice the traces of pictographs from the ancient character. The Han characters related to disease almost all have the form component " 疒 " , such as the combined characters " 病 bing (illness)" , " 疾 ji (disease)" , " 疗 liao (cure)", " 疼 teng (pain)" , and " 痛 tong (ache)". The category meaning of " 疒 " is "disease". Consider the form components " 衤" and " 礻 " as further examples. In writing, people often misuse the two components, such as incorrectly writing " 神 shen (god)" as " 袡 " or " 裙 qun (skirt)" as " 裠 ", because they do not know that " 礻 " indicates the category meaning of "sacrifice" and " 衤 " indicates the category meaning of "cloth", and in fact the pictographic elements of the two form components are different.

The Origin of the Category Meanings of Form Component " 疒 ": The form component " 疒 " describes a sick person lying on a bed.

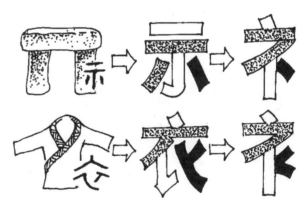

The Origin of the Category Meanings of Form Components " 衤 " and " 礻 ": The form component " 礻 " originated from the sacrificial alter used in an ancient sacrificial ceremony, and " 衤 " originated from the upper garment as worn in ancient times.

111

Category Meanings of Common Form Components

Form Components	Ancient Character Forms	Category Meanings	Form Components	Ancient Character Forms	Category Meanings
氵		Water and liquid	刂		Knives and using knives
口		Using one's mouth and the manner of speaking	马(馬)		Horses and that which is related to horses
扌		Hands and using hands	趵(足)		Feet and using feet
朰(木)		Woody plants and wood products	广		Houses
艹		Herbal plants	疒		Disease
亻		Person	页		Head
圠(土)		Land and building	粎(米)		Rice and grain
钅		Metal and metal products	酉		Wine and brewing products
纟		Silk and silk products	犭(犬)		Animals
月		Moon and body	衤		Clothes
女(女)		Women	飠		Foodstuffs
辶		Walking	礻		Gods and sacrifice
忄		Mentality and emotion	穴(穴)		Caves
日		The sun and time	彳		Walking and roads
灬(火)		Fire and high temperatures	灬		Fire and tail
石		Stone	鱼(魚)		Fish
心		Mentality and emotion	皿		Containers
竺(竹)		Bamboo and bamboo products	雫(雨)		Precipitation
讠		Speaking and language	羽		Bird's feather
贝		Money	衣		Clothing
宀		Houses	鸟		Birds
虫		Insects	冫		Ice and cold
禾(禾)		Seedlings of cereal crops	囗		Encircled
玊(王)		Jade and rarity	阝		(left) Earth mountain
屾(山)		Mountain ridges	阝		(right) City
目		Eyes			

The following are common form components (independent characters and their variants) in Han characters. Learning the forms and category meanings of these form components are extremely helpful if one wishes to learn combined characters.

Variants of Form Components. To make square forms balanced and beautiful, some form components have been changed to different positions. For example, when " 水 shui (water)" serves as a form component, it is written as " 水 " in the lower part of a character and as " 氵 " in the left part of a character, and when " 心 xin (heart)" serves as the form component, it is written as " 忄 " in the left part of a character and as " 小 " in the lower part. It is worth mentioning that many Han characters will change a little when serving as the left form component. For example, " 山 " is written as " 山 ", " 马 " as " 马 ", and " 女 " as " 女 " (see the table above). Regarding the variants of form components, " 手 shou (hand)" has the most variants and is used the most frequently, examples being " 又 ", " 寸 " and " 攵 ". Appreciating that they are " 手 " is very useful when learning Han characters.

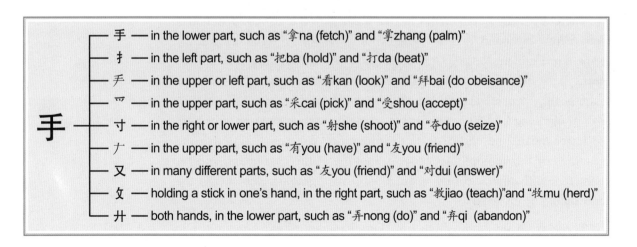

手

├─ 手 —— in the lower part, such as "拿na (fetch)" and "掌zhang (palm)"

├─ 扌 —— in the left part, such as "把ba (hold)" and "打da (beat)"

├─ 手 —— in the upper or left part, such as "看kan (look)" and "拜bai (do obeisance)"

├─ 爫 —— in the upper part, such as "采cai (pick)" and "受shou (accept)"

├─ 寸 —— in the right or lower part, such as "射she (shoot)" and "夺duo (seize)"

├─ 𠂇 —— in the upper part, such as "有you (have)" and "友you (friend)"

├─ 又 —— in many different parts, such as "友you (friend)" and "对dui (answer)"

├─ 攵 —— holding a stick in one's hand, in the right part, such as "教jiao (teach)" and "牧mu (herd)"

└─ 廾 —— both hands, in the lower part, such as "弄nong (do)" and "弃qi (abandon)"

The Use of Pictographic Elements in the Form of Han Characters

With regard to the modern Han characters, the remnants of some ideographically pictographic elements, i.e., the stroke symbols representing some meanings, which are not only helpful when we are recognizing pictophonetic characters, but also distinguishing homophones and characters with similar forms. Even in the eyes of someone who is comparatively proficient in Han characters, these pictographic characters are likely to make the Han characters a kind of wonderful visual symbols.

Form Indicates Meaning

There are many homophones in Han characters. We cannot distinguish them merely by sound, and the issue can only be solved by looking at the forms. For example, " 治 病 zhi bing" and " 致 病 zhi bing", the former means that a sick people gets rid of disease after healing , the latter indicates that a healthy people gets sick; and " 期中考试 qi zhong kao shi" and " 期终考试 qi zhong kao shi ", the former refers the midsemester examination, the latter means the end-of-term examination. We can distinguish the meanings of the homophones only by looking at the characters, and for characters with similar forms, distinction of pictographic elements in the form should be involved.

There are many homophones in Han characters. Let's see an article composing of homophones. Mr. Zhao Yuanren (1892–1982), a great Chinese philologist, wrote a magical essay in ancient Chinese with 91 characters, Shi Shi Shi Shi Shi (History of Mr. Shi Eating Lions). It tells the story of a poet named Shi who ate a lion. All the characters in the essay are pronounced "shi" and you will only hear the sounds of "shi shi shi" without any corresponding knowledge of the content, but the Han characters with abundant forms allow us to read an imaginative and interesting story. Put another way, it is a work of fiction that can only be read, not heard.

Mr. Shi saw a lion in a market.

施氏食狮史

石室诗士施氏，嗜狮，誓食十狮。
氏时时适市视狮。
十时，适十狮适市。
是时，适施氏适市。
氏视是十狮，恃矢势，使十狮逝世。
氏拾是十狮尸，适石室。
石室湿，使侍拭石室。
石室拭，氏始试食是十狮尸。
食时，始识是十狮尸，实十石狮尸。
试释是事。

Translation

A poet named Shi lived in a stone house and liked to eat lion flesh, and he vowed to eat ten of them. He used to go to the market in search of lions, and one day at ten o'clock, he chanced to see ten of them there. Shi killed the lions with arrows and picked up their bodies, carrying them back to his stone house. His house was dripping with water, so he requested that his servants proceed to dry it. Then he began to try to eat the bodies of the ten lions. It was only then he realized that these were in fact ten lions made of stone. Try to explain the riddle.

Visual Symbols

Han characters are a set of quite marvelous visual symbols, by means of which we can have association and some artistic conception when using these words, whether reading great works of literature or appreciating the beauty of fine calligraphy.

An excellent literary work can display some artistic conception and enable people to experience an aesthetic pleasure. Sometimes the Han characters, as the transmitters of great literary works, can strengthen or deepen our literary appreciation by the simple virtue of their own visual imagery.

" 同 舟 共 济 " is a common idiom. " 舟 zhou" is the pictograph of a small boat and the marks of some ancient pictographic characters can still be discerned. " 同 舟 tongzhou" means "sitting in the same boat". " 济 ji" has the "three-dot water", meaning "crossing a river". " 同舟共济 " means people sitting in the same boat to cross a river. This idiom implies that people make a joint effort and work together to overcome difficulty. In Chinese, another idiom " 风 雨 同 舟 " (风 feng means wind and 雨 yu means rain) has a strong pictograph and a similar meaning to " 同舟共济 ".

These beautiful lines reveal a fresh and tranquil artistic conception of the bright moonlight filtering through the branches of the pine trees and the clear spring water flowing and rippling over the pebbles. The ten characters present us with a distinctive visual image and constitute a touching and beautiful natural scroll by virtue of the structures of pictographic, indicative, associative-compound and pictophonetic characters and drawing-like forms.

With works known as fresh and elegant poems that enjoy far-reaching conception, Mei Yaochen (1002–1060), a famous poet in the Northern Song Dynasty (960–1127) was good at enhancing the artistic conception by making use of the image of Han characters. For instance, he has a poem

The visual images of the characters in such idioms as "同舟共济" and "风雨同舟" inspire the reader to understand and appreciate their meaning.

"明月松间照，清泉石上流 (the bright moon is shining among the pine trees and the clear spring water runs over the pebbles)" are the verses of the Shan Ju Qiu Ming (Dusk in the Mountain Residence in Autumn) by Wang Wei(701–761), a great poet of the Tang Dynasty.

says that " 鸦 ya 鸣 ming 鹊 que 噪 zao 鹳 guan 鸰 yu 叫 jiao", in which 5 characters successively with the radical " 鸟 niao (bird)"and 3 ones with the redical " 口 kou (mouth)". When appreciating this poem, one may feel as if in the world filled with various birds and inundated with chirp.

"Withered vines hanging on old branches, Returning crows croaking at dusk. A few houses hidden beyond a narrow bridge. And below the bridge a quiet creek running. Down a worn path, in the west wind, a lean horse comes plodding.The sun dips down in the west. And the lovesick traveler is still at the end of the world."

These are verses from a famous work Tian Jing Sha·Qiu Si (Thoughts in Autumn) by Ma Zhiyuan (1250–1321), a poet of the Yuan Dynasty (1206–1368). The first three verses show nine things by means of pictographic characters and constitute a desolate picture. The setting sun emphasizes the sadness of the traveler. Pictographic characters greatly enhance the artistic conception of the work.

Square Han characters are mysterious, and the pictographic elements hidden in their square forms are the great and wonderful mystery of these characters. Pictographic elements play a significant role in the learning and use of Han characters. Of course, putting excessive emphasis on their pictographic elements is not exactly practical with regard to their modern form because these forms are no longer pictographic. But the pictographic elements of the characters' forms are extremely helpful for us to learn and write Han characters, and we should make use of them.

When appreciating the poem" 鸦 ya 鸣 ming 鹊 que 噪 zao 鹳 guan 鸽 yu 叫 jiao", readers may feel as if in the world filled with various birds and inundated with chirp.

Artistic Conception of the Tian Jing Sha·Qiu Si (Thoughts in Autumn), a Poem of the Yuan Dynasty.

119

HAN CHARACTERS AND CHINESE LANGUAGE

Characters are created after emergence of language, and the Han characters were written symbols created for recording the Chinese language.

Han characters are the basic structural units with which the Chinese language is recorded. They keep high consistency with Chinese language, and enjoy flexible word-formation with property beyond dialect and times, demonstrating their uniqueness and superiority.

Han Characters Adapt Themselves to Actual Chinese Language

Han characters quite adapt themselves to actual Chinese language with high consistency with it. It seems that their only difference lies in "appearance" and "pronunciation", namely, it is Han character upon seeing, and it is Chinese language upon reading out.

Han Characters Adapt Themselves to Chinese Language Dominated by Monosyllable

Chinese language is the language with monosyllable as the basic unit. In general, a syllable signifies a monosyllabic word or a morpheme (such as " 人 ren (person)" and " 物 wu (object)" in the disyllabic word " 人 物 ren wu (figure)"). Most of characters in ancient Chinese language were monosyllabic characters, such as " 学 xue (study)" and " 习 xi (review)", both of which can be separately used. In the saying "Learn and often review and practice, and is this not very happy?" from Confucius, the two characters are separately used to express two different meanings. In modern Chinese language, although most words are disyllabic, one syllable expresses one morpheme with fairly clear boundaries between syllables; for example, the disyllabic word "xuéxí" is combined by two morphemes including "xué" and "xí" and written as "学习 xue xi (study)".The boundary between the two characters (morphemes) " 学 xue (learn)" and " 习 xi (review)" is that between the two syllables "xué" and "xí". Apparently, one character shoulders one syllable, expressing the pronunciation of one monosyllabic word or one morpheme in Chinese language. One character correspondingly matches one syllable without any confusion, for example, there are 8 syllables in the sentence of "Wǒ zài Zhōngguó xuéxí Hànyǔ", which is written as " 我在中国学习汉语 wo zai zhong guo xue xi han yu (I learn Chinese language in China)", exactly 8 characters correspondingly matching 8 syllables.

Han Characters Adapt Themselves to Formless Chinese Language

Chinese language is a formless language without change in form, to which the Han characters adapted. In a language with changes in form, many words often change their forms, such as "a book" and "two books" in English. The consonant phoneme "s" may be used to express plurality in English, and "book" here changes its form into "books" either in pronunciation or writing. There is no such form change in Chinese language; in either " 一本书 a book" or " 两本书 two books", " 书 shu (book)" has no change in form neither pronunciation nor writing; it always pronounces "shū" and is written as " 书 book".

Han Characters Adapt Themselves to Chinese Language with Numerous Homophones

Homophones are quite common in Chinese language. Due to graphic form and structure, Han characters extremely adapt themselves to this feature of Chinese language. Han characters can definitely distinguish the

meanings of those characters with same pronunciations such as "师 (teacher), 狮 (lion), 尸 (corpse), 施 (apply), 诗 (poem), 湿 (wet), 失 (loss)" (they all pronounce "shi" in Chinese language).

战士——战事	因为——音位	雨露——语录	绘画——会话
上级——上集	复数——负数	图画——涂画	世纪——事迹
舒适——书市	经历——精力	独立——独力	销售——消瘦
意义——意译	考察——考查	石油——食油	报酬——报仇
蜜蜂——密封	世界——视界	形式——形势	有利——有力

Examples of homophones. These characters have same pronunciations but different meanings, and can only be distinguished by their forms.

In sum, Han characters quite adapt themselves to actual Chinese language with high consistency with it. It seems that their only difference lies in "appearance" and "pronunciation", namely, it is Han character upon seeing, and it is Chinese language upon reading out.

Han Characters Are the Basic Structural Units in Chinese Language

Since monosyllable is the basic unit of Chinese language, then the Han character with monosyllable is necessarily the basic structural unit in Chinese. To be specific, sentences in Chinese language are formed by syllables one after another, which are formed by characters (morphemes) one after another in writing, namely, sentences are formed by character, words and phrases, and words formed by characters constitute phrases, so character is the basic structural unit in a sentence, and lays a foundation for a sentence structure. To take the sentence " 我在中国学习汉语 wo zai zhong guo xue xi han yu (I learn Chinese language in China)" as the example again, this sentence has 8 syllables and is formed by 8 characters, among which 6 characters constitute three disyllables " 中国 zhong guo (China)", " 学习 xue xi (learn)", " 汉语 han yu (Chinese language)", and two small phrases including " 在 中 国 zai zhong guo (in China)" with preposition – object structure and " 学习汉语 xue xi han yu (learn Chinese language)" are grouped based on the three disyllables, then big phrase " 在中国学习汉语 zai zhong guo xue xi han yu (learn Chinese language in China)" is combined to constitute a complete sentence " 我在中国学习汉语 wo zai zhong guo xue xi han yu (I learn Chinese language in China)" eventually. The smallest or basic structural unit in this sentence is the 8 Han characters (morphemes) including " 我 wo, 在 zai, 中 zhong, 国 guo, 学 xue, 习 xi, 汉 han, 语 yu". In simple terms, Han characters rather than the words are the basic structural units in Chinese language.

Han Characters Have Strong Word-formation Ability

Han characters have incredibly strong word-formation ability, which can enable you to express more words with fewer characters.

Flexible Word-formation

Han characters have fairly flexible word-formation ability with which almost every character may constitute many words. To take the character "学 xue (learn)" as example, plenty of words such as "学习 xue xi (learn)", "学校 xue xiao (school)", "学生 xue sheng (student)", "学问 xue wen (knowledge)", "学分 xue fen (credit)", "学历 xue li (education background)" can be formed with "学 xue (learn)" being the first character in a word, and words such as "自学 zi xue (self-study)", "教学 jiao xue (teaching)", "数学 shu xue (math)", "讲学 jiang xue (lecture)", "勤学 qin xue (studious)", "留学 liu xue (study abroad)" etc. can be formed with "学 xue (learn)" being the last character in a word. For another instance, now that "治水 zhi shu (tame flood)" (e.g., "大禹治水 Da Yu zhi shui (Yu the Great tamed the flood)") can be combined, then "治山 zhi shui (mountain governance)", "治田 zhi tian (field governance)", "治湖 zhi hu (lake governance)", "治海 zhi hai (sea governance)", "治病 zhi bing (treatment)", "治安 zhi an (public security)", "治理 zhi li (governance)", "治疗 zhi liao (therapy)" and so on can also be combined; Words or phrases can seem to be infinitely combined like this. There are more than 1,300 syllables in Chinese language, but hundreds of thousands of words are recoded as Han characters, which is a convincing proof for the flexible word-formation ability of Han characters. This feature of Han characters may inevitably cause numerous homophones such as " 学生 xue sheng (student)" and " 学笙 xue sheng (learn Sheng (a kind of musical instrument))", " 治病 zhi bing (treatment)" and " 致病 zhi bing (cause disease)", " 治理 zhi li (governance)" and " 至理 zhi li (famous dictum)". However, relying on the graphic form and structure with ability to distinguish, the Han characters can definitely distinguish them. In addition, same characters in different positions within words may constitute words with different meanings, such as 国 王 guo wang (king)—— 王 国 wang guo (kingdom), 蜜 蜂 mi feng (bee)—— 蜂蜜 feng mi (honey), 生 产 sheng chan (parturition)—— 产 生 chan sheng (produce), 进行 jin xing (conduct) —— 行进 xing jin (march forward), 科学 ke xue (science) —— 学科 xue ke (subject), 害虫 hai chong (pest) —— 虫害 chong hai (insect attack), 黄金 huang jin (gold)—— 金黄 jin huang (golden yellow), etc. All examples above can illustrate fewer characters can be used to express more words in Chinese language.

It is not hard to see that, such flexible word-formation ability of Han character is based on its graphic feature, and every character in disyllabic words or polysyllabic words presents its own meaning. The meanings of a disyllabic word are often the combination of meanings of the two characters consisted of it. For example, " 国王 guo wang" means king of a county but " 王国 wang guo" means a county managed by a king; " 金黄 jin huang" means the color of yellow like gold; " 变成 bian cheng" means "changing into"; " 注重 zhu zhong" means "looking out and paying attention to"; " 增光 zeng guang" means "adding luster to". Such is the case of polysyllabic word, for instance, " 电视机 dian shi ji" means the electric visible machine.

The flexible word-formation ability of Han character demonstrates its graphic function and its basic role for Han language.

Easiness in Word-formation

It is hard for learners to memorize words one by one in alphabetic writing. For example, the words "pork, beef, mutton, chicken, fish" in English are respectively written as " 猪肉 zhu rou, 牛肉 niu rou, 羊肉 yang rou, 鸡肉 ji rou, 鱼肉 yu rou". Apparently, it is easier to recognize and write these Han Characters than these English words because we just need to add the names of these animal before the character " 肉 rou (meet)", and if more names of animal are memorized, more similar words can be successfully written. Moreover, there are twelve words for the twelve months in a year in English including "January, February, March…December", which needs a period of time for memorization, however, in Chinese language, as long as we add the characters indicating the twelve numbers before the character " 月 yue (month)", we can easily remember the twelve months which are written as " 一月 yi yue(January), 二月 er yue (January), 三月 san yue (March)… 十二月 shi er yue (December)". Likewise, it is easily to write out a number of words with the character " 月 yue (month)", such as " 岁月 sui yue (time and tide), 日月 ri yue (sun and moon), 蜜月 mi yue (honeymoon), 圆月 yuan yue (full moon), 残月 can yue (waning moon)". This word-formation feature of Chinese language shows that, grasping some frequently used characters is strongly convenient for future use.

Han Characters Have the Property beyond Dialects and Times

Numerous peoples speaking different dialects in China use the same kind of written language; some today's Chinese can recognize Jiaguwen [inscriptions on bones or tortoise shells of the Shang Dynasty (1600– 1046 BC)]. Such property beyond dialects and times possessed by Han characters is indeed a miracle in the history of civilization of the world.

There are many dialects varying considerably in Chinese language. To take " 书 shu (book)" as an example, it pronounces "shū" in Mandarin, "sū" in Sichuan Dialect, "xū" in Hubei Dialect, but collectively written as " 书 shu (book)"; " 街 jie (street)" pronounces "jiē" in Mandarin but "gāi" in Southern Fujian Dialect, Sichuan Dialect and Shanghai Dialect; " 鞋 xie (shoe)" pronounces "xié" in Mandarin but "hái" in Sichuan Dialect and Hunan Dialect, etc.; " 肉 rou (meat)" pronounces "ròu" in Mandarin but "yòu" in Shandong Dialect. Due to different pronunciations in different dialects, people from different areas in China often do not follow each other's dialect; however, they all use Han characters which help them to understand each other at the sight of the Han characters. Even if it is hard to read some Han characters or some people are unaware of how to read them, they also may get the meanings through character patterns, which indicate Han characters' property beyond dialects. The Han characters' property beyond dialects helps them break through the barriers of different dialects, and ensures ordinary contacts and cultural communications of people across China. Hence, Han characters have been the unified written communication tool used in the whole country.

Meanwhile, Han characters have the property beyond the times. The currently used Han characters gradually evolved from the ancient Han characters, today's people can still read all books written by Han characters and preserved from the ancient times, and basically read the jiaguwen from 3,000 years ago. And reading books with the history of more than one thousand years is rather difficulty for a people using alphabetic writing. Such property beyond times enables Han characters to create a miracle in the history of written language and civilization of the world. The Han characters play an important role in continuing Chinese civilization for 5,000 years to be the only uninterrupted civilization continued up to now in the world.

It is difficult for people from different regions in China to communicate with each other in dialects. But if they use square Han characters, all the people can understand.

"Sinosphere"

The time-honored and wonderful square Han characters are not only the core of Chinese culture, but also the symbol of Oriental Civilization, and the subsistent "Sinosphere" is exactly one of illustrations.

The "Sinosphere" is a concept of culture put forward by the Japanese scholar, which is also referred to as the "East Asian cultural Sphere" or "Confucian world". It refers to the historical or current countries or regions with Han characters as the tool to spread language and the cultural carrier. Its major features lie in similarity in culture, historical influence by Han culture and Confucianism in particular, completely use of Han characters in the past or at present, or mixed use of Han characters with native characters, such as extensive use of words from ancient Chinese language in native languages, etc. The leading feature of "Sinosphere" is the use of Han characters. The strong impact of Chinese culture and Han characters on surrounding countries and regions fundamentally formed the "Sinosphere".

"Sinosphere" is a kind of cultural transmission phenomenon, which is formed through a long and complicated historical process. The major region of "Sinosphere" is undoubtedly China, which is the birthplace of the Han characters with main members of DPRK, South Korea, Japan, Vietnam and other China's surrounding countries and regions that use or used Han

characters. Singapore, Malaysia and other Southeast Asian countries are also members of the "Sinosphere".

Korean Peninsula

DPRK and South Korea, China's northeastern neighbors, are jointly called "Goryeo" in ancient times. Koreans use Korean but without character originally. Around the 1st century BC, Han characters were introduced into the Korean Peninsula; in the early 5th century, Han characters are popularly learned and used in various countries on the Korean Peninsula. In 1444, Korean Sejong the Great issued the Hunminjeongeum (lit. The Correct/ Proper Sounds for the Instruction of the People) that created the Korean alphabet "Hangul", which was a kind of phonetic alphabet created with

The doorways are often decorated with couplets written in Han characters to welcome the spring In Seoul, South Korea.

strokes of Han characters and used in conjunction with Han characters. Even when the Korean alphabet was prevailing, writing articles and poems completely with Han characters was still rather prevalent.

After World War II, DPRK and South Korean respectively declared independence, and successively abolished Han characters to use the alphabetic writing – Hangul. Later on, DPRK and South Korea launched educations for Han characters in succession, for example, South Korea restored to use parts of Han characters. There are quite a few Han characters and words in Korean. According to some statistics, Han characters and words in Korean reach about 60%, either in a spoken or written way. Currently, there are increasingly Han characters and Chinese language learners in South Korea and DPRK. The world's first "Confucius Institute" was established in Seoul, Korea, which is an organization designed to promote Chinese language and spread Chinese culture.

Japan

It is an eastern neighbor of China, which was called "Dongying" "Fusang" "Woguo" in the ancient times. The Japanese originally used Japanese without characters, later on Han characters were introduced to Japan together with the ancient books and records written by Han characters, and became the official language of Japan. In the 3rd century AD, The Analects of Confucius and other Chinese books and records were introduced into Japan on a large scale. The Nihon Shoki (or The Chronicles of Japan) appeared in 720 AD is a Japanese history book written with Han characters. In the late 8th century, in order to cope with the inconvenience caused by the fact language and characters were used for different purposes, Japan created simplified cursive font of Han characters to mark the "hiragana" in Japanese pronunciation, and then created simplified components of Han characters to mark the "katakana", and eventually formed the "kanji-kana mixed style" in which kanji and kana were jointly used.

After World War II, Japan began to limit the numbers and use of Han characters, and promulgated a series of Han characters lists such as the tōyō kanjihyō (literally, List of Kanji for General Use) with 1850 words, and jōyō kanjihyō (literally, Regular-Use Han Characters) with 1945 words, etc. The kanji-based "kanji-kana mixed style" that used for a thousand years changed into the kana-based "kana-kanji mixed style". In order to facilitate writing, Japan simplified the Han characters. On the one hand, they absorbed the fonts of simplified characters in ancient China, such as " 学 xue (learn), 虫 chong (insect), 旧 jiu (old), 礼 li (etiquette), 麦 mai (wheat), 当 dang (when)"; on the other hand, they made some changes in accordance with writing habits of its people, such as " 黒 (黑 hei (black)), 海 (海 hai (sea)), 器 (器 qi (device)), 突 (突 tu (suddenly)) , 徳 (德 de (moral)), 歩 (步 bu (step))" and other characters. Japan attaches great importance to the education of Han characters in terms of character leaning, calligraphy, and study. For example, Japanese scholars have made great contributions for researches on ancient Han characters and jiaguwen.

Vietnam

It is a southern neighbor of China, which was called "Jiaozhi" in ancient times. According to historical records, the "Xiang County" set

Japan collects a representative Han character nationwide every year to show the important events that has taken place in this year. The annual Han character of 2013 is " 轮 ".

in the period of First Emperor of Qin included the current northern and central Vietnam; Emperor Wu of Han set the County in Vietnam in 112 AD. Vietnam had no character initially until Han characters were introduced into Vietnam, then Vietnamese absorbed a number of vocabularies from Chinese language. In a fairly long period of history, Han characters were used as the official characters of Vietnam. In order to better express the Vietnamese national language, the Vietnamese gradually created a kind of new character – Chữ nôm from about the 11th century, which were use together with Han characters. Chữ nôm was a kind of semi-phonetic and semi-graphic character, which was essentially a kind of Han characters-based square character.

In the late 19th century, the French colonialists vigorously promoted Latin alphabetic writing in Vietnam, which then officially became the commonly used "Chữ Quốc Ngữ" (the Vietnamese alphabet, literally national language) in 1945 in Vietnam with Han characters and Chữ nôm no longer used. Nevertheless, we see that, the modern Vietnamese absorbed many elements of Chinese language, which is outstandingly shown in terms of Chinese loanwords. According to statistics, Chinese loanwords account for more than 60% of the total Vietnamese vocabulary.

Currently, Vietnam re-focuses on learning and use of Han characters and Chinese language that has become the second foreign language in Vietnam; many universities set up department of Chinese Language and Literature, and tens of thousands of Vietnamese students study in China.

Singapore

It is a city-state in the Southeast Asia, where aboriginal people use of Malay without use of Han characters since ancient times. With the large number of Chinese entered in the 19th century, Han characters and relevant culture were introduced into this island country. Now in Singapore, the

Shop Sign in Han Characters on the Singapore Street

Chinese with Chinese language as the mother tongue account for 3/4 of the entire population. Singapore's official language is English, Mandarin, Malay, and Tamil. It implements the education system that Chinese language and English are used simultaneously. It is noted that, with regard to use of Han characters, Singapore is promoting simplified Han characters. Its Table of Simplified Characters is totally consistent with China's Complete List of Simplified Characters. Now, the simplified Han characters are widely used in newspapers, books, textbooks, test papers in universities and middle and primary schools, advertisements, websites, television subtitles in Singapore. Calligraphers and painters also like to use simplified characters for their creative work.

Malaysia

It is located in Southeast Asia with a great many Chinese. As with Singapore, Malaysia is also heavily promoting Pinyin and simplified Han

Nowadays, there are increasing Chinese language and Han characters learners around the world.

characters with the idea of that "this is the new trend of the development of Chinese culture" and "simplified characters are scientific". The Table of Simplified Characters promulgated by Malaysia is also entirely identical to the Complete List of Simplified Characters promulgated by China.

The "Sinosphere" marked by Han characters is a real cultural existence worthy with strong vitality, and its history and current situations deserve our researches, and its future prospects are more worthy of our expectations.

CHINESE HISTORY NARRATED IN HAN CHARACTERS

History is not only the succession of dynasties but is also a lively and vivid subject composed of stories from real life.

The uniqueness of Han characters is that many look like historical and cultural pictures involving images and stories, as well as the wisdom and philosophy of our ancient ancestors at the time of their creation.

Social Life in Ancient Time

Just as a fossil makes us aware of some otherwise hidden aspect of the primeval world, so the square Han characters can also disclose some secrets from the past. The earliest formation of Han characters was based on the thoughts and understanding of our ancient ancestors as they reflected on the world around them, as well as the day-to-day social life at that time. Therefore, the forms of many ancient Han characters can be viewed as historical and cultural pictures, revealing some truth about our past. In fact, they may be even more reliable than some of the research conducted by various historians. As "living fossils", Han characters tell us many things…

A Unique Understanding of the World

The period of about 10,000 to 4,000 years ago was the Neolithic Age, and what historians refer to as the time of "remote antiquity". During this period the human race developed with extraordinary rapidity and laid the foundations of our civilization fruits, but, on the other hand, our early ancestors were powerless in the face of the forces of nature. They could only contend against these by evoking the aid of magic. The ancient Han characters represented their initial understanding of the world around them and are a unique conception of our earliest Chinese ancestors.

The Stone ware made by primitive people (Paleolithic Age)

昔

Kaishu

Jiaguwen

Jinwen

Xiaozhuan

昔

In Jiaguwen " 昔 xi" was an associative-compound character composed of " 水 shui (water)" and " 日 ri (sun)", indicating that time (日) flows like a river (水) and meaning the past, such as the phrases " 昔日 xiri (in former days)" and " 往 昔 wangxi (in former times)". But if we conduct some serious research into the original meaning of "former days" and think back to the remote time when characters were first being created, we will find that it is not as simple as we first thought. It can be imagined that in the memories of our ancestors the Flood might be the event that left the deepest impression. Ancient Chinese legend " 大 禹 治 水 Da Yu zhi shui (Yu the Great tamed the flood)" told people such a big flood, while western story Noah's Ark also described the horrible image that the flood inundated the whole world. In the light of this, we can view the character " 昔 " as a pictographic character. It vividly tells us: there was the time of a great Flood in remote antiquity.

The Picture of Dayu Regulating Rivers and Watercourses (Stone rubbings of the painting of the Eastern Han Dynasty). It's said that ancient hero Dayu led people to excavate the mountains and dredge channels to fight against flood. After 10 years' hardworking, they finally eliminated the flood.

Formation of Character " 昔 xi (past)": Huge Flood Covering the Light of Day. Archaeological science has confirmed that a huge flood really took place in the world 4,000 years ago.

天

In Jiaguwen the character " 天 tian (heaven)" looked like a standing person facing the viewer. The head of the person was given especial prominence, so the original meaning of " 天 " was "top of head" and it also indicated the sky above. The sky is boundless, and ancient people called it " 苍天 cangtian (boundless sky)". " 天 " also generally refers to the cycle of nature, and many natural things incorporate the character " 天 ", such as " 天文 tianwen (astronomy)", " 天象 tianxiang (astronomical phenomena) ", " 天气 tianqi (weather)", " 天然 tianran (natural)", and " 春天 chuntian (spring)", " 秋天 qiutian (autumn)", " 今天 jintian (today)", and " 明天 mingtian (tomorrow)", etc. The sky is high above us, and is where we see the sun, moon and stars, and also the source of wind, rain and thunderstorms. Ancient people could not understand these natural phenomena and thought the sky was a magic, omnipotent and supreme god, so they called it " 天神 tianshen (sky god)", " 天帝 tiandi (sky god)", and " 上天 shangtian (heaven)". In ancient China there was a saying that "the sky is round and the earth is square". The Temple of Heaven in Beijing was the place where the emperors of the Ming (1368–1644) and Qing (1616–1911) Dynasties offered sacrifice to heaven. The buildings were all rounded in shape and had blue roofs symbolizing the sky. In order to enhance their prestige, the emperors ruling the world of men used " 天 " to refer to themselves, thus assuming the name " 天子 tianzi (son of the heavens)".

But the sacred sky also had its own troubles. In ancient China there was a popular fairy tale Nv Wa Bu Tian (Nu Wa Mended the Sky). It is said that in remote antiquity there was a big hole on the sky, so the world was caught up in disorder and floods, fire, and ferocious animals, making life impossible for the people. Later, a grand goddess named Nv Wa, with a woman's head and the body of a snake, fired five-color stones and mended the the hole in the sky, restoring peace to the world. This story reflected

Picture of Nv Wa Mending the Sky

Kaishu

Jiaguwen

Jinwen

Xiaozhuan

The Temple of Heaven in Beijing

ancient people's fear of the sky and showed their strong desire to alter and conquer the natural world. It is worth while giving some thought to the fact that today the global climate is becoming warmer and warmer and the major cause of our abnormal climate is a big hole in the ozone layer above the South Pole. This scientific fact is very similar to the ancient Chinese people's understanding of nature.

地

Kaishu

Xiaozhuan

Compared to " 天 tian (sky)", " 地 di (earth)" has a closer relationship with human beings. People's two feet are anchored to the earth, what they eat and use are all of the earth, and " 地 " seems like a mother giving birth to everything, so there developed the character " 地 " indicating these meanings.

" 地 " is an associative-compound character. The left component is
" 土 tu (dust)" and the right component is " 也 ye (also)". In respect of the
origin of characters, " 也 " represents the female (According to the *Shuowen
Jiezi* by Xu Shen, " 也 " refers to the private parts of a woman). With the
combination of " 土 "to form the character

" 地 ", it indicates that the " 地 " seems like a mother and is the dust
from which everything originates. " 大地母亲 dadimuqin (mother earth)" in
common parlance indicates the meaning.

" 地 " opposes " 天 ", the sky is above and the earth is below, and
ancient people said that they came into being at the same time. In ancient
China there was a popular fairy tale Pan Gu Kai Tian Pi Di (The Creation
of the Sky and the Earth by Pan Gu): Long ago the universe in which we
live was a Chaos. One day, a man named Pan Gu raised his huge ax in
order to cleave it. With a tremendous crash, the Chaos was broken. Those
things which were light and clear rose up to form the sky, and the heavy

Picture of Pan Gu Creating
the Sky and the Earth

The Taishan Mountain, in the East High Mountain. From the time of Emperor Qinshihuang
of the Qin Dynasty, many emperors would climb the Taishan Mountain to hold sacrificial
ceremonies to the heaven and the earth and such activities were known as " 封禅 fengshan".

and dirty things descended to form the earth. The sky rose up every day, the earth deepened every day, and Pan Gu standing between the two became taller and taller with every sunrise. He was afraid that the sky and the earth would join together again, so he used both of his hands to support the sky and planted his feet on the earth for 18,000 years. By this time the sky was very high and the earth was very deep, and Pan Gu, having exhausted all his energy, fell to the ground and expired. Thus the sky and the earth came into being.

Chinese people venerate the sky and the earth. Ancient emperors held sacrificial ceremonies to the sky and the earth on the Taishan Mountain. The Temple of Heaven and Temple of Earth in Beijing were where the emperors of the Ming (1368–1644) and Qing (1616–1911) Dynasties held sacrificial ceremonies to the sky and earth. On their wedding day, a couple will also "拜天地 baitiandi" (do obeisance to the heaven and the earth) and which has therefore become another word for wedding in China.

A Comparison Between the Character "人 ren (person)" and Other Characters Indicating Animals in Jiaguwen: "人" stands upright, but animals do not. The characters in the picture are drawn from up to down: 人 ren (person), 豕 (猪)shi (pig), 虎 hu (tiger), 马 ma (horse), 龙 long (dragon), 犬 quan (dog), 象 xiang (elephant), 兔 tu (rabbit), 鼠 shu (mouse), 鱼 yu (fish), and 龟 gui (tortoise).

人

"人" is a pictographic character. In Jiaguwen and Jinwen it represented the profile of a standing person with outstretched arms. The simple strokes show the ancient ancestors' observational ability and their understanding of themselves. The ancient form of the character "人" omitted all the details of a human body and focused on the standing-up legs and outstretched arms which distinguish us from other animals – we can walk upright and use our hands to make and hold tools. In addition, the character depicted a standing figure, but at that time the characters indicating animals in Jiaguwen, such as "虎 hu (tiger)", "马 ma (horse)", "龙 long (dragon)", "犬 quan (dog)", "象 xiang (elephant)", "鼠 shu (mouse)", and "龟 gui (tortoise)", almost all had downward turning tails and legs bending to the left, with the exception of " 鹿 lu (deer)", " 牛 niu (ox)", and " 羊 yang (sheep)". It seems quite clear that ancient people differentiated themselves from animals in aspect of the characters' forms and gave prominence to the important position held by themselves in the scheme of nature, i.e. "man is the soul of all things" to quote a common saying.

There is a philosophy of "the combination of heaven and man" in ancient China. Let's see the character " 天 ", it is obvious that " 人 " is a part of " 天 ". Heaven is above, the earth is below, and man is situated between the two. In ancient times, heaven, earth and man were referred to as the "three talents", which showed that ancient people blended man into nature and essentially identified themselves with the natural world. It is actually the reflection of an ancient philosophy – "the combination of heaven and man".

Beijing Man Some 500,000 Years Ago. They were able to stand up, make and use tools with their hands and bake food by means of fire.

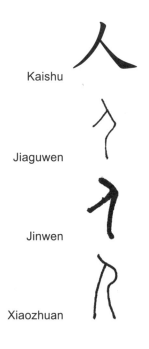

Kaishu

Jiaguwen

Jinwen

Xiaozhuan

神

In primitive society, the powers of nature were a constant threat, and so these people invested many natural things with supernatural power. When creating the Han characters that represented these natural forces, people lived in a state of constant fear and tried hard to indicate such supernatural power, for example in the characters " 神 shen (god)" and " 鬼 gui (ghost)". And the formation of the character " 神 " is the most representative.

In the minds of our ancient ancestors, the gods were omnipotent supernatural spirits and managed the sky and the earth. In Jiaguwen the

Formation of the Character " 神 shen (God)": Two large and mysterious hands are extended towards the heaven and the earth.

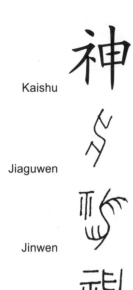

Kaishu

Jiaguwen

Jinwen

Xiaozhuan

character was an "s"-shaped curve connecting the two. The upper part looked like a huge hand reaching out to the sky and the earth, mysterious and awesome. It is the character " 申 (𝓈)shen", the original form of the character " 神 ". With careful observation, you will see that the "S"-shaped curve looks very much like the lightning in the sky during a thunderstorm. Lightning was also, back then, a mysterious and awesome thing, so " 神 " probably originated from people's fear of it. Many philologists say that " 申 " is the original character of " 电 ".

In fairy tales and religious texts, gods are the creators and masters of everything in the world. They have limitless supernatural power and are literally awesome. In ancient China people believed in many gods, such as the God of Heaven, the God of Earth, the Grain God, Pan Gu, Nv Wa, the God of the Sun, Yuhuang Dadi (Jade Emperor), Wang Mu Niang Niang (Queen Mother of the West), the God of the Kitchen, and the Square God. They were all important gods in ancient times. Many people believed that their souls would continue to exist after their death, and these invisible souls were also regarded as gods.

Head of Clay Goddess Sculpture in Hongshan Culture, which is, so far, deemed as the earliest goddess sculpture found in China. The Hongshan Culture can trace its history back to c. 5,000 to 6,000 years ago.

Pious Totem Worship

Totem worship was a very common phenomenon in social life of humans. Totem means "his kindred", as well as blood, race, group. People in the primitive society tended to believe that some kinds of animal, plant, or natural objects had kinship with their own clans, thus marked their own clans with these things, i.e., totems. People relied on, worshiped, sacrificed their own totems to seek for protection, which was what we called "totem worship". In the earliest time of creating characters, Chinese people directly adopted the totem signs of clans, so some Han characters have left us with a reliable testimony of primitive totem worship. Now let's take the character " 龙 long (dragon)" as an example.

Nine-Dragon Wall in the Imperial Palace in Beijing (the Ming and Qing dynasties). These nine dragons were imperial dragons with five claws.

Big Jade Pig-headed Dragon from the Time of the Hongshan Culture

Kaishu

Jiaguwen

Jinwen

Xiaozhuan

龙

"龙 long (dragon)" is the most magic totem in China and can be truly called the "No.1 Totem in China". "龙" is a pictographic character. There are many forms of character "龙" in Jiaguwen and Jinwen. They usually had a thin body, horns on the head, and a widely open mouth. In Kaishu, the complex form of "龙(龍)" seems to have become totally symbol. But there are still some pictographic elements: the left part is the dragon's head, while "立" is the dragon's horns and "月" is the dragon's mouth; and the right part is the dragon's body.

The Chinese dragon has a very strange shape. It does not exist in the natural world and was the product of people's imaginations. It is believed by archaeologists that the Chinese dragon was a totemic integration, with the snake as its principle inspiration. It has the body of a snake, the head of a pig, the horns of a deer, the ears of an ox, the beard of a goat, the scales of a fish, and the claws of an eagle. The image of the Chinese dragon reveals to us a historical truth: in remote antiquity the Huaxia Clan in the Yellow River Valley had the snake as its totem, and under the leadership of the Yellow Emperor, it conquered and formed alliances with other clans and formed a huge united tribe. The Huaxia Clan's principle totem – the snake – became combined with the totems of other clans – pig, deer, ox, sheep, fish and eagle – to form a composite totem of the Huaxia Clan, i.e. the dragon totem. The clan alliance of the Huaxia Clan later developed into the Chinese nation. Archaeologists have unearthed a dragon made of shells from an ancient tomb in Henan Province, and it is the earliest dragon in China, being some 6,000 years old. It is known as the "No.1 Dragon in China". Many beautiful jade dragons have also been discovered among the ruins of the Hongshan Culture, which flourished 5,000 years ago. They all imply that dragon worship was prevalent in remote antiquity.

Different from the Western dragon breathing fire, the Chinese dragon spat water from its mouth. It could cause wind and rain in the heavens. China is an agricultural country and people always wish for favorable weather and a good harvest, so in ancient times there were temples dedicated to the dragon king everywhere in China. People would go to these temples in time of drought and pray to the dragon to bring rain. Therefore the dragon symbol was the direct result of Chinese agricultural civilization.

Dragon is the most important totem in ancient China. Since the Western Han Dynasty (206 BC–24 AD), it was exclusively possessed by the emperors for 2,000 years. These emperors declared themselves as "True Dragon and Son of Heaven" with the dragon as their symbol, which was a means to raise their prestige by virtue of dragon's divinity. In the Imperial Palace of Beijing (or Forbidden City) where all emperors in nearly 500 years before 1911 lived, carved dragons and dragon drawings can be seen everywhere and 12,654 dragons can be found just in one hall named "Hall of Supreme Harmony". What a "dragon world" it is!

Nowadays, the dragon has been one of Chinese people's favorite mascots from an ancient totem and symbol of imperial power. The dragon in today's China has another kind of new meaning, which is the symbol of Chinese people's spirit of soaring upward, and the symbol of Chinese nation composed of more than 1.3 billion people.

Eternal Ancestor Worship

The ancestor worship of Chinese people began in the days of patriarchal clan communities. It was believed by ancient people that ancestors gave them life and the souls of these ancestors' could protect their children, so they would worship their ancestors and make sacrifice to them. Ancestors are the basis for the continuation of clans or individual human beings, and such knowledge meant that ancestor worship has prevailed for thousands of years in China, right up to the present day, and exceeds the worship of divinities.

Mausoleum of the Yellow Emperor in Shaanxi. The Yellow Emperor is the ancestor of the Chinese nation. On the occasion of the annual Qingming Festival, a grand sacrificial ceremony would be held there.

Shi Zu (lithoidal male genital organ) from Shang Dynasty.

祖

Knowing the formation meaning of " 祖 zu(ancestor)", you will understand the essence of ancestor worship radically – ancestors are the basis for the continuation of both clans and their individual members.

In Jiaguwen the character was written as " 且 " and in Jinwen a component " 礻 " was added. " 祖 " means ancestor, i.e. the elder generations of a clan or a family, especially the those in the remote past. For example, "the Yellow Emperor and the Yan Emperor are the ancestors of the Chinese nation". According to the *Shuowen Jiezi*, " 祖，始庙也 (' 祖 ' is the temple where sacrificial ceremonies for ancestors are held)". It clearly referred to ancestors. " 礻 " in the character indicates worship and sacrifice, and so what does " 且 " indicate? It is the memorial tablet for sacrificing ancestors' souls and the symbol of those ancestors, as a pictographic character of " 土 tu (clay)", from which everything is initially created, and ancestors have tens of thousands of descendants, or it can be seen as a representation of genitalia, by means of which children are conceived. In remote antiquity the phallic worship on " 祖 " was very widespread and many pottery, stone and wood " 祖 " survive from this time. Comparing these three sayings, the last might more closely correspond to the essence of ancestor worship expressed in the old saying "ancestors are the root of the continuation of clans and their individual members" and closer to the time that ancestor worship came into being in the patriarchal clan community. Same as " 宗 zong (ancestral temple)", the formation of character " 祖 " not only expressed ancient Chinese people's respect, worship and offering of prayers to their ancestors, but also reflected nature worship and the worship of genitalia.

Chinese people very much respect, even worship, their ancestors. They will follow the names of fathers, call their father's father " 祖 父 zufu (grandfather)" and their mother's father " 外 祖 父 waizufu (maternal grandfather)". These are all customs left over from the primitive patriarchal clan society. Some Chinese people spend their whole lives doing gigantic tasks in order to add luster to their ancestors, i.e. " 光宗耀祖 guangzongyaozu (bringing honor to one's ancestors)".

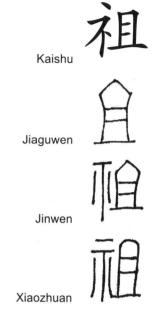

Kaishu

Jiaguwen

Jinwen

Xiaozhuan

Show of Ancient Civilization Sights

Photos and pictures are real records of things. Some Han characters, like pictures, recorded the evolution of ancient civilization and are extremely vivid, realistic, lively and interesting. We can learn a great deal about history and culture by means of characters, and Han characters provide the best opportunity of doing so. They are truly a wonder among the characters of the world! Han characters indicate meanings by forms. Drawing-like characters reveal a significant amount about the emergence and development of ancient civilization in China.

Evolvement of Ancient Substantial Civilization

In remote antiquity, Chinese society witnessed stages of development that progressed from fishing and hunting to the raising of livestock, and from gathering to agriculture. Some ancient Han characters, like pictures and photographs, remain as vivid records of these various stages of development.

Fishing and hunting were important activities in the early history of human beings. At the end of the primitive society the rock paintings in China and the cave mural paintings in Europe have left us with a great deal of information, but Han characters tell us even more.

渔

"鱼 yu (fish)" is a noun. This ancient character was pictographic, with head, body and tail, just like the shape of a fish. "渔 yu (fish)" is a verb and refers to the activities related to fishing. The Banpo Ruins in Xi'an where people lived 6,000 years ago are ruins of typical matriarchal villages. Many excavated items of earthenware are painted with beautiful fish, and many fishing nets and hooks and other fishing tools have also been discovered, which indicate that fishing was an important activity at that time. In Xiaotun Village, Anyang, Henan Province, where Jiaguwen were unearthed, many fish bones were also excavated, including those of cyprinoid, grass carp, and mackerel. These were all fish that were commonly eaten at that time. Jiaguwen left some characters related to fishing, such as " 𤋮 (渔)" and " 𝄜 (网 wang(net))". It indicates that in the Shang Dynasty (1600–1046 BC) 3,000 years ago, fishing witnessed a further development. Among these characters, " 渔 " is the most interesting. It originally meant fishing and now is a pictophonetic character with the components of " 水 shui (water)" and " 鱼 yu (fish)". But in Jiaguwen it was an

Picture of Fishing of the Shang Dynasty. In Jiaguwen the character " 渔 yu (fish)" showed several fishing methods 3,000 years ago.

Pottery Basin Painted with Man-face Fish Pattern (Yangshao Culture Period). The pattern of man-face fish on painted pottery was the totem of the Banpo Clan.

渔
Kaishu

Jiaguwen

Jinwen

Xiaozhuan

associative-compound character with many forms. In the picture, these four Jiaguwen characters of " 渔 " reflected at least three kinds of fishing current at that time: catching fish by hand, fishing with hook and line, and fishing with a net. The fourth form was " 渔 " which is still in use today. With an appreciation of the Jiaguwen characters of " 渔 ", we do not just learn about the fishing methods of olden days, but also acquire important historical information: in and before the Shang Dynasty (1600–1046 BC) fishing had become one of the most important sources of people's daily food, and fishing itself had become comparatively common production activity at that time.

Shooting Wild Animals

 逐

In Jiaguwen the character " 逐 zhu (chase)" was an associative-compound character and originally meant chase. The upper part of the character represents a pig (豕 shi) and the lower part is the feet of a person (止). The form of the character vividly indicates that a wild boar is running and a hunter is chasing closely after it. A hunter was chasing after a wild boar, i.e. hunting and killing a wild animal. In Jiaguwen there was a

Kaishu

Jiaguwen

Jinwen

Xiaozhuan

The Ancient Rock Painting Chasing and Shooting Yaks in Qinghai. It was a painting by Chinese people that was made 10,000 years ago, and gives a genuine idea of hunting wild yaks at that time.

character " 射 she (shoot)". The form shows a hand drawing a bow. What will the arrow be aimed at? Of course, some wild animals. In Jiaguwen there are many characters describing the hunting of animals. For example, " 网 ()wang (net)" indicates fishing and hunting, " 敢 (敢)gan (bold)" shows a hand holding a three-pronged spear (which later evolved to a trap) to capture a wild boar face on, " 坠 (墜 分 zhuì) (fall)" shows chasing after and trapping a wild boar, " 罗 (羅 ꞔ)luo (catching birds with a net)" depicts using a net to catching birds, and " 获 (獲 ꞔ)huo (capture)" shows the capture of a bird by hand. The animals hunted by people in early times can also be found in Jiaguwen, such as " 鹿 lu (deer)", " 野牛 yeniu (wild ox)", " 野猪 yezhu (wild boar)", " 兔 tu (rabbit)", " 马 ma (horse)", " 虎 hu (tiger)", " 熊 xiong (bear)", " 鱼 yu (fish)", and " 鸟 niao (bird)". In Jiaguwen there were many characters depicting animals, indicating the close relationship between ancient people and that which they hunted, caught, and ate.

采

Gathering was the first stage in the evolution of agriculture. Before the emergence of agriculture, gathered wild plants were the people's most important source of food. According to the ancient Chinese fairy tale Shen Nong Tasted Hundreds of Herbs, "Shen Nong tasted hundreds of herbs and discovered 72 poisonous varieties in one day." This little anecdote describes the gathering of wild plants in the olden days. In Shi Jing (Classics of Poetry), the first anthology of poems in Chinese history, there are many vivid descriptions of this activity. This collection activity must surely have been recorded in the Han characters, and the character " 采 " is the most direct description. It is an associative-compound character. In Jiaguwen the upper part of the character was a hand and the lower part was a tree bearing

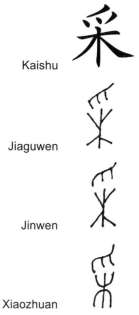

Kaishu

Jiaguwen

Jinwen

Xiaozhuan

Picture of Collecting Mulberry Leaves (Pattern on the Bronze Ware of the Warring States Period)

fruit. The two components formed the meaning of "picking". In Jinwen the fruit on the tree were omitted and the character in Kaishu style evolved from Xiaozhuan.

In ancient China the art of agriculture developed and matured very early. "Founding the country on the basis of agriculture" has always been the national policy of China, and the Chinese people have always understood the most simple truth, i.e. that "people's lives depend on food". Therefore, the ancient culture in China was, to a great degree, agricultural. Even now,

Shen Nong Tasted Hundreds of Grasses and Herbs

Shen Nong, namely the Yan Emperor, was the sun-god in ancient Chinese mythologies. According to the legend, he had ox-head but snake-body, taught people to make farm tools, drill wells for getting water, plant the five cereals (rice, two kinds of millet, wheat and beans), who was the representative in China's collection and farming stage. The story that Shen Nong tasted hundreds of grasses and herbs was most widely spread. It was said that, people still ate weeds, berries and small insects, drink unboiled water when stepping into the farming stage, which often sickened and poisoned them, so Shen Nong risked his life to personally tasted all the grasses and herbs as well as springs, so as to tell people what things were edible or inedible. During which, he found some crop varieties as well as tea, herbs, etc. Shen Nong was said to have been poisoned by 72 kinds of plants in a day and eventually died from the poison, he tasted the Gelsemium elegans with strong toxicity, and die from rotten intestines. Shen Nong is a figure in ancient times who earned extraordinary respect from Chinese people.

farmers still account for the majority of the population. Then, what does the character " 农 nong (agriculture)" that Chinese people are the most familiar with actually mean?

China is a major agricultural country. It is not only abundant with a whole variety of crops but also has an excellent tradition of intensive cultivation. This intensive cultivation is reflected in various aspects, such as the use of agricultural implements, ways of planting, field management, and the cultivation of crops. They are all fully represented in ancient Han characters. In these characters " 田 tian (field)" looks like a field, " 耒 lei (plow)" and " 耜 si (plowshares)" look like farming implements that are used to turn up the soil, " 利 li (sharp)" indicates the shearing of grain, " 犁

Kaishu

Jiaguwen

Jinwen

Xiaozhuan

井 jing (well)
the form of a water well with a square mouth

井 jing (well)
the form of a water well with a square mouth

耒 lei (plough)
a tool to plough with tynes at its end

耜 si (spade-like plough)
a spade-like plough

疆 jiang
measure fields by means of a bow

苗 miao
seedlings are growing in the fields

焚 fen (burn)
start a fire to reduce the grass on waste land to stubble

楚 chu
enter the forest to fell trees

力 li
sharp-headed ploughing implement

刀 dao (knife)
a tool to cut logs

斤 jin
axe-shaped tool to cut wood

耕 geng
ploughing a field with the plough in both hands

秦 qin
take hold of a pestle and pound rice

利 li
harvest crops with a scythe

奉 feng
hold tree seedlings in one's hands

留 liu
dig out channels to irrigate fields

艺 yi
a person is planting seedling with both hands

协 xie
three persons sowing together

封 feng
plant a seedling with both hands

秉 bing
hold a seedling in one's hand

Examples of Jiaguwen Describing Farming Activities

Creation of the character of " 香 xiang (delicious)": It consisted of the character " 黍 shu (millet)" and the character " 甘 gan (sweet)", which means sweet and delicious rice made of millets. Then the character " 黍 shu (millet)" was simplified into the character " 禾 he (cereal)" and the character " 甘 gan (sweet)" into the character " 日 ri (sun)".

li (plow)" gives us the impression of a plow being drawn by an ox, " 耤 ji or jie (plough)" indicates furrowing the soil with a hand-plow, " 协 xie (joint)" shows three people together plowing a field, and " 留 liu (stay)" indicates drawing water to irrigate fields. In the view of Chinese nations, mature of crops is the most beautiful scene, and grains are the most fragrant. Even the name of Qin Dynasty (221–206 BC) means good havest of grains. The characters " 秀 xiu (beautiful)" , " 香 xiang (fragrant)" and " 秦 qin (name of a dynasty of china)" all have " 禾 he (ripened grain)" with the meaning of grains.

Then, what does " 农 " mean? It originally meant hoeing up weeds or harvesting. In Jiaguwen, the character's upper part was " 草 cao (grass)" and " 木 mu (tree)" indicating grains, and the lower part was " 辰 chén (辰)", i.e. the pictograph of holding a stone harrow in both hands. In Jinwen " 田 tian (field)" was added between the " 草 " and " 木 ", so that the meaning became more clear: people were hoeing up weeds or harvesting in the field with stone harrows. Were they engaged in agricultural activity? After the change of Lishu, the upper part was combined into " 曲 ", and the character was written as " 農 " (the complex form of the character " 农 "). The stone haft was the tool with which people hoed up weeds and harvested back in the days of remote antiquity. It is obvious that the character " 农 " appeared very early.

耤

The character " 耤 ji or jie (plough)" in jiaguwen vividly depicts a picture that a man with " 耒 lěi (an ancient plough)" in two hands was plowing the land by treading such plough with his feet. A big foot was portrayed under the figure of human to demonstrate treading such plough into the land depend on strength of feet. " 耒 lěi" is an ancient tool to turn the soil with long hand and double toothed gears. People shall tread it with feet when plowing land with it. The character " 耤 ji or jie (plough)" is a proof that tools like " 耒 lěi" have been used for farming in Shang Dynasty (1600–1046 BC). Jinwen (inscriptions on ancient bronze ware) added a string of pictographic symbols under this character to express rows of plowed fields, and then the meaning of plowing land was more explicit. In Xiaozhuan (the lesser seal style Chinese characters of the Qin Dynasty (221–206 BC)), " 耒 lěi" was placed in the left to depict holding such plough with two hands, and that string of pictographic symbols was placed in the right and changed into " 昔 xi" . Now, the character " 耤 ji or jie (plough)" has

Kaishu

Jiaguwen

Jinwen

Xiaozhuan

Father (Oil painting, Luo Zhongli). This famous modern oil painting portrayed honest and modest image of Chinese famers who work hard in the fields for generations.

been less used in terms of plowing, which was replaced with the character " 耕 geng (plough)" . In fact, " 耕 geng (plough)" is evolved from " 耤 ji or jie (plough)" with the left part kept but the right part simplified into " 井 jing (well)" .The character " 耤 ji or jie (plough)" in jiaguwen vividly depicts a picture that a man with " 耒 lěi (an ancient plough)" in two hands was plowing the land by treading such plough with his feet. A big foot was portrayed under the figure of human to demonstrate treading such plough into the land depend on strength of feet. " 耒 lěi" is an ancient tool to turn the soil with long hand and double toothed gears. People shall tread it with feet when plowing land with it. The character " 耤 ji or jie (plough)" is a proof that tools like " 耒 lěi" have been used for farming in Shang Dynasty (1600–1046 BC). Jinwen (inscriptions on ancient bronze ware) added a string of pictographic symbols under this character to express rows of plowed fields, and then the meaning of plowing land was more explicit. In Xiaozhuan (the lesser seal style Chinese characters of the Qin Dynasty (221–206 BC)), " 耒 lěi" was placed in the left to depict holding such plough with two hands, and that string of pictographic symbols was placed in the right and changed into " 昔 xi" . Now, the character " 耤 ji or jie (plough)" has been less used in terms of plowing, which was replaced with the character " 耕 geng (plough)" . In fact, " 耕 geng (plough)" is evolved from " 耤 ji or jie (plough)" with the left part kept but the right part simplified into " 井 jing (well)".

Kaishu

Jiaguwen

Jinwen

Xiaozhuan

艺

" 艺 yi" was originally an associative-compound character formed by " 人 ren (human)" and " 木 mu (wood)" in both Jiaguwen and Jinwen, which vividly signifies that a man plants seedling with two hands and kneeling on the ground, and there is soil in some patterns. The Xiaozhuan

basically remained the character pattern in Jinwen with slight changes in the shape of seedling. In the later Kaishu, the character was added by the component " 艹 " on the upside, and added by " 云 yun (cloud)" at the bottom, which was written as " 藝 ". The original meaning of " 艺 yi" was "planting". The old saying " 树艺五谷 shu yi wu gu", meant planting the five cereals. The ancients believed that planting trees required skills and experience, and thus extended the meaning of this character to "skill", just as in words like " 园艺 yuan yi (gardening)", " 工艺 gong yi (craft)" etc. Its meaning also was extended to the meaning of " 艺 yi" in word " 艺术 yi shu (art)", such as the word " 六艺 liu yi (six arts)" which was the educational content of ancient nobles including rites, music, archery, chariot steering, calligraphy and arithmetic. The word-formation of "Art" shows that, the ancient people have taken plantation as a very important life skill and ability. The simplified character " 艺 yi" has become a pictophonetic character with the form-component of " 艹 " and the sound-component of " 乙 yi".

Formation of the Character " 年 nian (year)": A person carrying a sheaf of grain on his back. The original meaning of " 年 " is mature of grains, indicating harvest.

年

Is " 年 nian (year)" only a noun indicating time? No. In China it is redolent of the country's agricultural culture.

" 年 " has direct relationship with agriculture. In Jiaguwen and Jinwen, the character's upper part was " 禾 he (ripened grain)" and the lower part was " 人 ren (person)", and the whole form looked like a person carrying a sheaf of grain on his back, indicating harvest. In the *Shuowen Jiezi*, " 年 " was explained as "grain becomes ripe". In other word, the original meaning of " 年 " is harvest. During the Shang (1600–1046 BC) and Zhou (1046–256 BC) Dynasties, people called grains obtained by hardwork in one year " 受年 shounian" . At that time grain ripened once a year, so its meaning was extended to " 岁 sui (year)" . One " 年 " is one " 岁 " . In the Temple of

年

Kaishu

Jiaguwen

Jinwen

Xiaozhuan

Heaven, the place where emperors of Ming Dynasty(1368–1644) and Qing Dynasty(1616–1911) to worship the god, the largest building is "Qinian (祈 年) Palace" . " 祈年 " is praying for favorable weather, and praying to the gods to grant the people a good harvest.

" 年 nian (year)" is also related to the Chinese people's traditional festival – the Spring Festival which is also called "过年 guo nian (celebrating the Spring Festival)" . It derives its origin from the "December sacrifice" in Shang Dynasty of 3,000 years ago. " 腊 la (12th month of lunar month)" is an ancient sacrifice activity, in which the laboring people offered sacrifices to the gods in heaven, gods in hell and ancestors at each twelfth month of the lunar year after harvests based on hard work. The Spring Festival is China's oldest and most important folk traditional festival, so if you want to understand the thoughts and feelings and customs of the Chinese people, you'd better celebrate a Spring Festival together with them.

" 过年 guonian (spend the Spring Festival)" is called "spring festival", which is the most important Chinese festival.

163

Marriage and Family

Marriage and having a family is one of the most important components of our civilization. The ancient Han characters have, by their forms, left us with much knowledge in this respect.

We first look at the character " 女 nv (female)" , a pictographic character. " 女 nv (female)" in Jiaguwen depicts a cross-handed woman kneeling on the floor. Like painters, the ancestors created this character depicting the physical characteristics of women and even personalities only with two concise lines: the upper crossed lines showed their plump breasts, and the below curved lines drew their fat hips, and the whole image looked so calm and gentle. It is amazing that such superb abstraction ability appeared 3,000 years ago.

In the long course of human history, woman firstly led their sons and daughters to arduously march in the ancient land, which opened the door to civilization — human stepped into the matriarchal society. In the matriarchal society, thriving clans rely on women's child-bearing, and their food was mainly from plants collected by women and livestock fed by women. Men's fishing and hunting activities at that time often can not be guaranteed, so the status of women was very high. With the advent of the agrarian age, men with stronger physical strength became the major producers and women more commonly stayed home — humans began to enter the patrilineal clan society in which the character " 女 nv (female)" was created.

The character " 女 nv (female)" is also an important component that constitutes plenty of characters. Some have favorable meanings, such as " 好 hao (good), 娇 jiao (delicate), 妙 miao (wonderful), 娟 Juan (graceful)"

Formation of the Character " 女 nv (female)": A cross-handed woman kneeling on the floor.

Kaishu

Jiaguwen

Jinwen

Xiaozhuan

and other characters representing goodness and praises for women; some have unfavorable meanings, such as " 奴 nu (slaves), 婪 lan (greed), 奸 jian (evil), 妖 yao (demon)" and other character expressing contempt for women.

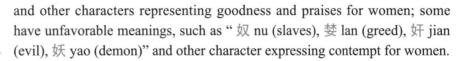

安

" 安 an (stability)" provides us with another picture of the stage of group marriage within the clans of a maternal society and has great cultural value.

Formation of the Character " 安 an (safety)": An adult woman is quietly kneeling down in her house, and feeling calm and peaceful.

Kaishu

Jiaguwen

Jinwen

Xiaozhuan

It is an associative-compound character. In Jiaguwen, the outer part of the character was the form of a house and the inner part was a kneeling woman. Here we see a woman quietly kneeling down in a house, giving people an impression of stability and placidity, which was the original meaning of the character " 安 ". A woman in a house implied that she was married and had formed a family and could thus lead a stable life. But from the point of view of culture, this character gives us a further insight. " 安 " is an old character and its formation reflected the ancient maternal clan society and a kind of marriage condition that specified that "only mothers

Restored model of house in Banpo Neolithic Village, Xi'an, Shaanxi. The Banpo historical site is a typical historical village site of matriarchal society in the Yellow River Basin, enjoying a history of around 6,000 years.

165

were known and fathers were unknown". In the later period of this type of society, marriage was no longer kept inside a clan but could be extended beyond it (spouse marriage). An adult woman could receive a man outside the clan and would have to leave her childhood home. An adult woman in possession of a house had her own "family" and would feel contentment, which made the whole clan more stable.

婚

The character " 婚 hun (marriage)" is written as the character " 昏 hun (dusk)" in jiaguwen. The character " 昏 hun (dusk)" is an associative-compound character composed of " 人 ren (human)"and " 日 ri (sun)" , indicating that the sun fell below human's arm and it was already dark. In ancient times, marriages were carried out after dusk, which were exactly "marriages by capture" . That is because, during the transition from the matriarchal clan society to the patrilineal clan society, in order to ensure the patrilineal continuation, men did not go to women's tribes any more but required women to live at their homes, so that children gave birth by these women were certainly their own children which deserved to inherit their properties. In this case, women would lose their power and status in the matriarchal clan society and consequently revolted such marriages. To deal with such revolts, men had to capture women to obtain marriages by use of force. To make a successful capture, they had take actions in the dark, so such actions after dusk were called " 昏 hun (dusk)" . So as to make a more specific definition, " 女 nǚ (female)" (form-component) was later added beside " 昏 hun (dusk)" (sound-component), which was how the pictophonetic character " 婚 hun (marriage)" was made. The current character " 婚 hun (marriage)" has already lost its original meaning and marriage is now entirely a very happy thing.

Formation of the Character " 婚 hun (marriage)": The action of seizing a woman by force after dark.

Kaishu

Jinwen

Xiaozhuan

Formation of the Character " 家 jia (house)": There is a pig in a house.

Kaishu

Jiaguwen

Jinwen

Xiaozhuan

 家

After establishing settled-down lives, people began to think of family, and in fact the idea of family must have appeared very early. The form of the character " 家 jia (house)" is very strange, but nevertheless a true record of the situation as it was during the emergence of ancient houses and their occupants' knowledge of how to build a home.

" 家 " is also an old character. In respect of form, it is an associative-compound character. Under the " 宀 " there is a " 豕 (猪) (pig)", i.e. there is a pig in the house. What does it mean? Formerly, back in the days when people had only just started to establish settled homes and families, fishing and agriculture became more sophisticated, resulting in an abundance of game and grain, and people began to raise animals. They raised pigs, cattle, sheep, dogs, chickens and horses, and these are the "six livestock" as referred to by ancient people. Pigs were both the most prolific and the most important of these livestock, being both a major foodsource and a symbol of wealth and social position. In Chinese museums you can see that very often pig bones were included in the graves of ancient clan heads, and those occupying very high positions might have had dozens of

Black pottery bowl with pig pattern in Hemudu Culture, proves that the people in the Neolithic Age have begun to raise animals such as pig.

pigs buried alongside them. At that time, by having a house and raising pigs, people could live and had " 家 ". Archaeologists have discovered many houses in the ruins of remote antiquity, and the upper part was for people and the lower part was for raising pigs. These combined dwellings for both people and livestock might be represented as " 家 ".

孝

Formation of the Character " 孝 xiao (filial piety)": A child is helping an elder along the walkway.

" 孝 xiao (filial piety)" was one of the most advocated moral standards in ancient feudalist society. Respecting and serving well one's parents is " 孝 " or " 孝顺 xiaoshun (filial piety)" . " 孝 " is an interesting associative-compound character. In Jiaguwen, the lower part of the character was " 子 zi (baby)" and the upper part was something like grass. The meaning is not exactly clear. It might mean that children wore flowers and grass on their heads and played games to amuse elders. In Jinwen, on the other hand, the meaning of the character " 孝 " was very clear. The upper part of the character was an old man with a crookback and very little hair, and the lower part was a child, meaning the child supported or carried the old man on its back. It was actually an act of respect towards one's elders and demonstrated a kind of filial piety, and this is the original meaning of the character. Confucius advocated " 孝 " and regarded it as the finest thing within a family. He said " 弟子入则孝 ", meaning children must show filial piety to elders in their family. But ancient people focused more on " 顺 shun (obedience)" than " 孝 ", children had to obey their parents and elders no matter whether what they said was right or wrong, otherwise those children would be condemned as impious. However, today, the meaning of " 孝 " doesn't highlight absolute obedience. But showing filial piety to one's parents and elders is still a virtue, as well as an important social moral standard. People not showing such respect to their parents and elders will not be respected in China.

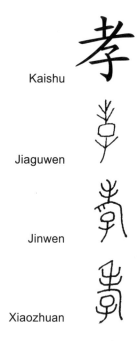

Kaishu

Jiaguwen

Jinwen

Xiaozhuan

The Cruelty of War

" 战争 zhanzheng (war)" is a terrible monster, but in the long history of the human race, it has occurred all too frequently. The ancient history of China also witnessed countless wars. Han characters recorded the history of war and some even described its cruelty.

 戈

" 戈 " was a common weapon during the Shang (1600–1046 BC) and Zhou (1046–256 BC) Dynasties 3,000 years ago. The character " 戈 " is a pictographic character. In Jiaguwen the character " 戈 " gives an accurate description of the form of such a weapon: there was a long pole, and the extended cross line above was the blade. In Jinwen, the character became more specific. The blade surmounting the shaft seemed more like a dagger and at the base of the pole there was a fork that could be inserted into the ground. " 戈 " appeared very early, and archaeologists have discovered many stone " 戈 " in the ruins of the later period of the Neolithic Age. They might well be the axes that were used back then to fell trees. During the Shang (1600–1046 BC), Zhou (1046–256 BC), Spring and Autumn Period (770–475 BC), and Warring States Period (475–221 BC), the head of " 戈 " was mostly made of bronze and there were two kinds, i.e. short-pole and long-pole " 戈 ". The short-pole " 戈 " was used by infantrymen in hand-to-hand fighting, and the long-pole " 戈 " by charioteers, and its length could be as much as three meters. In the Western Han Dynasty (206 BC–25 AD), due to the rise in popularity of iron ware, " 戈 " gradually disappeared from the battlefields and its place was taken by another weapon, named " 矛 máo (spear)".

The weapon " 戈 " appeared very early, as did the character representing

Bronze Battle-axe (the Spring and Autumn Period)

Kaishu

Jiaguwen

Jinwen

Xiaozhuan

it, so all the characters related to weapons and war include the form of "戈", such as "戊 wu", "戉 (yue)", "戌 (xu)", "戎 (rong)", "戒 (jie)", "戍 (shu)", "成 cheng", and "我 wo". In Jiaguwen "戊", "戉", and "戌" were all the images of a battle-axe, "戒" was a defensive position in which a battle-axe is held in both hands, and "戍" meant taking guard under a battle-axe. "我" was originally a serrated weapon, and later it was loaned to indicate "oneself". Many other characters related to weaponry and warfare include "戈", such as "战 zhan (fight)", "武 wu (military)", "戚 qi (a kind of axe)", and "國 (国) guo (country)". Almost needless to say, "戈" has become a radical indicating a weapon or war.

Formation of Character " 伐 fa (cut down)": A battle-axe is being violently brought down on a person's neck.

伐

In Jiaguwen the character of " 伐 fa (kill)" was an associative-compound character with clear meaning. The right part was " 戈 " and the left part was " 人 ", and the blade of the battle-axe was cutting a man's head off. It is a terrible picture! Therefore, the original meaning of the character was "chop and kill" – chop one's head off! Its meaning was extended to " 攻 打 gongda (attach)", "讨伐 taofa (crusade against)", and "征伐 zhengfa (go on a punitive expedition)".

People would be killed in " 征伐 ". In fact, countless soldiers died in major and minor " 征 伐 " in Chinese history! During the Warring States Period (475–221 BC) the Qin State went on a punitive expedition against the Zhao State and engaged its forces in Changping, Shanxi. Both sides experienced terrible losses. The army of the Zhao State was completely annihilated, and the soldiers of Qin also took heavy casualties. On the battle field, " 尸横遍野 shihengbianye (a field littered with corpses)" and " 血流 漂 杵 xueliupiaochu (so much blood being shed as to float the pestles)"… This is the most tragic and disastrous battle in the history of China, " 长

Kaishu

Jiaguwen

Jinwen

Xiaozhuan

平 之 战 the battle of Changping". It was estimated that at least 600,000 soldiers died on the battlefield – this is " 伐 "!

As a verb, " 伐 " is often used regarding such matters as felling trees, for example " 伐木 famu (fell trees)" , " 采伐林木 caifa linmu (deforest)" , and "砍伐树木 kanfa shumu (cut down trees)". But the picture of "chopping a person's head off with a battle-axe" as shown by the form of " 伐 " always reminds us of the relationship between it and wars.

The Art of War

The Art of War is a famous ancient Chinese book and the world's first book on military strategy, which attributed to Sun Wu (c. 535 BC–?) in the State of Qi in the late Spring and Autumn period. It describes in some detail the principles of strategy and tactics, stresses to know yourself as well as the enemy in a combat, highlights the importance of the concentration of troops against the enemy, and emphasizes to attach importance on wars but avoid making wars at random. It marks the maturity of ancient Chinese military thinking.

In Jiaguwen, the character of " 弓 gong (bow)" was pictographic and a real drawing of a bow. There was a complete bow with a curved line on the left as the bow itself and a straight line on the right as the bowstring. There was an additional line on the bow. It was a decoration, and a thread could be tied on it and then also tied to the arrow. Thus the arrow could be easily retrieved after being released. This kind of early bow was called " 弋 (yi)" and was used in fishing and hunting. In Jiaguwen there were another character of " 弓 " . Just like subsequent characters, another character of " 弓 " had only the bow without the bowstring.

The former was usually made of flexible bamboo or wood. The arrows were mostly made of bamboo, so the character " 箭 jian (arrow)" has a form component of " 竹 (𣲘) (bamboo)" . In ancient times people called an arrow " 矢 (shi)" . It is also a pictographic character and is written as " 𠂤 " in Jiaguwen. Its front end indicates the arrowhead, and the two crossed lines below represent the feathers at the end of the arrow shaft. A weighty arrowhead means the arrow can fly faster and further, and increases its killing power. The feathers at the end can balance the shaft and make the flying arrow steadier and more accurate.

The Han character "射 she(shoot)" was extended from " 弓 " and " 箭 ". In Jinwen, the character " 射 " was the image of a person drawing his bow to shoot an an arrow. The orginial meaning of " 射 " was shooting arrows. However, the bow generally became " 身 shen (body)" and hand became " 寸 cun (1/3 decimeter)".

The people in ancient China paid a great deal of attention to archery. In

Kaishu

Jiaguwen

Jinwen

Xiaozhuan

Picture of Shooting Bird of the Warring States Period (pattern on the bronze ware). An archer is shooting a flying bird with an arrow attached to a slender thread, and the arrow can be recovered.

the time of Confucius, accurately shooting arrows was viewed as one of the "six skills" at which any person serving the state must be adept. Bows and arrows played a major role in ancient battles and there were many instances where their use proved decisive. Nowadays, of course, we don't see bows and arrows on the battlefield. But archery is still a popular pastime, and is represented in the Olympic Games.

In ancient times the most flexible item in a warrior's armory was a " 盾 dun (shield)". In combat, a soldier held a battle-axe (or spear, or sword) in one hand and his shield in the other. He could both attack and defend, and his battle effectiveness was consequently strengthened.

In Jiaguwen " 盾 dun (shield)" was a pictographic character representing a shield. In Jinwen, the character had become an associative-compound character. The upper part was a person and the lower part was a shield, indicating a person holding a shield to defend himself. The earliest shields were made of wood covered with animal hide. Later they were made of metal. Today we can see many excavated ancient metal shields.

In ancient China there was a story about a spear and a shield: in the Chu State a man was selling weapons. He held up the shield and cried out, "This shield is the hardest and no spear can pierce it." Then he held up the spear and cried out, "My spear is very sharp and it can pierce any shield." Then a bystander addressed him thus, "If I used your spear to pierce your shield, what would be the result?" The man selling weapons had no answer, even after thinking for a long time. Later, people began to use the phrase " 矛盾 " to indicate mutual contradiction.

Bronze Shield of the Qin Dynasty

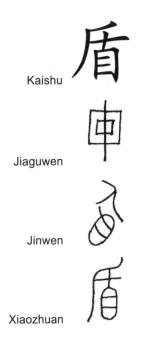

Kaishu

Jiaguwen

Jinwen

Xiaozhuan

173

Daily Life

The formation of many Han characters originated from the daily life of ancient people. Clothing, food, shelter and means of travel are the basic necessities of ordinary life, and there are many Han characters that represent these things.

Dragon Robe in the Qing Dynasty

"衣 yi (clothing)" is a pictographic character. In Jiaguwen, Jinwen and Xiaozhuan, the character was a vivid drawing of the ancient outer garment. The upper part was the collar, the lower part was the garment itself, and the empty spaces on either side were the sleeves. Now Chinese people refer to clothing as "衣裳 yishang" but in ancient times they were two words. "衣" referred to the upper outer garment in the form of the ancient character form of "衣", and "裳" (the ancient form was "常") referred to the lower skirt. In olden days there was a saying that "the upper is '衣' and the lower is '裳' (pronunciation is "chang")". People wore long garments with wide sleeves and skirts, no matter male or female. There was also another kind of clothing combining the upper garment and skirt, i.e. "深衣 shenyi". Trousers did not appear until later and were introduced to the Han people by northern nomadic tribes. These nomadic people lived on the plains, and trousers were more suitable for riding on horseback. Robes were bulky and awkward, but trousers were far more practical. The emergence of

Woman's Dress of Han Dynasty: 深衣 shenyi

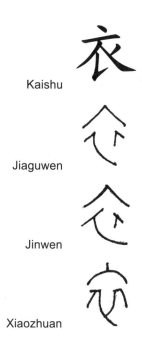

Kaishu

Jiaguwen

Jinwen

Xiaozhuan

trousers was a revolution in the cultural history of Chinese costume.

From the time of Jiaguwen in the Shang Dynasty (1600–1046 BC) to the Qing Dynasty (1616–1911) there were extremely colorful types of ancient dress in China, but they were basically in the form painted by the character " 衣 ". We can actually say that the style of " 衣 " determined the trend of Chinese costume for some 3,000 years. When used as a form component, the character " 衣 " is written as " 衤 " on the left or below, and when it is on the right, it is still written as " 衣 ". The characters having " 衣 " as their form component are mostly related to dress, such as " 衬 chen (underwear)", " 衫 shan (sleeveless jacket)" , " 袄 ao (fur garment)", " 袍 pao (gown)", " 裙 qun (skirt)" , " 裘 qiu (fur coat)" , and " 装 zhuang (outfit)". With careful observation, you will see that the component " 衤 " was clearly changed from " 衣 ", and the left-falling and right-falling strokes on the right of the character " 衣 " are the two dots on the right of " 衤 ".

Kaishu

Jiaguwen

Jinwen

Xiaozhuan

Since ancient times, food has been the first necessity of Chinese people. Due to Chinese people's deep love and huge attention paid to food, China is famous all over the world for its food culture.

" 食 shi (food)" is an associative-compound character. In Jiaguwen, the lower part of the character was a cooking vessel full of food, the two dots above indicated that this food was about to boil over, and the triangle at the top represented the lid of the cooking pot. Such a vessel was used to contain rice, Chinese sorghum, and millet. When used as a noun, it indicates food, such as " 主食 zhushi (staple food)" and " 冷食 lengshi (cold drinks and snacks)" ; and when used as a verb, it indicates the action of eating, such as the phrases " 食肉动物 shirou dongwu (meat-eating animals)" and " 废寝

忘食 feiqin wangshi (forget food and sleep)" . " 食 " is a radical character, and all the characters with " 食 " as their components are mostly related to "food" or "eating", such as " 饭 fan (rice)" , " 饼 bing (cake)" , " 饮 yin (drink)", " 饿 e (hungry)" , and " 饱 bao (full)" .

By the time of Jiaguwen, the culture of food and drink had become more developed. Let us take just bronze ware as an example. " 鼎 ding" was a vessel for boiling meat, " 甑 (zeng)" was a vessel for steaming food, " 簋 (gui)" was a container for staple foodstuffs, " 尊 zun" was a container for wine, and " 爵 (jue)" was a cup for drinking wine. These characters indicating vessels can all be found in Jiaguwen. Consider another example. Both Jiaguwen and Jinwen had the character " 酉 you (wine)" . It not only represented the earthenware jug in which wine was contained, but also referred to the " 酒 jiu (wine)" for drinking. In the *Shuowen Jiezi*, 67 characters have " 酉 " as their components, showing that the wine culture in China has a long history. In Jiaguwen many characters have components of " 食 shi (food)" , " 火 huo (fire)" , " 禾 he (ripened grain)" , " 米 mi (rice)", " 肉 (月)rou (flesh)" , " 羊 yang (sheep)" , " 酉 you (wine)", and " 皿 min (vessel)" . They constitute an abundant and colorful series of characters related to food and drink. These characters not only indicate that Chinese food culture has a long history, but also reveal the most important truth about China, a vast and still largely agricultural country, " 民以食为天 (Food is the first necessity of the people)".

Complete Manchu-Han Banquet. " 满汉全席 manhan quanxi (complete Manchu-Han banquet)" became popular during the Qing Dynasty. It contained 108 dishes and was eaten over three days, which continues to be a special part of Chinese food and drink culture.

住

Chinese architecture has a long history and a distinctive national style, and holds an important position in the world history of architecture. From the footed houses in the southern Hemudu Cultural Ruins and the shallow cave-houses of the northern Banpo Ruins in the remote past, to the Imperial Palace buildings of the Ming (1368–1644) and Qing (1616–1911) Dynasties, Chinese architecture has a history of some 7,000 years. Generally speaking, ancient Chinese architecture was characterized by a wooden structure, wide roof, and the layout of a planar complex. The Imperial Palace in Beijing, with which we are all familiar, demonstrates these characteristics, which in turn were recorded by Han characters. These characters have form components of " 宀 ", " 穴 xue (cave)", " 土 tu (earth)", " 木 mu (wood)", " 广 guang (wide house)", and " 户 hu (house)" and are almost all related to buildings. For example, " 宀 " is the outer form of a house with

Kaishu

住

Xiaozhuan

住

Hui-school Civilian Houses in Anhui

Taihe Hall in the Imperial Palace in Beijing. Taihe Hall is an example of typical architecture with a wooden structure and a wide roof. The complex of the Imperial Palace is a typical example of planar layout.

wooden pillars on two sides and sharply pointed roof on top. The characters indicating dwellings usually use it as their form component, such as " 家 jia (home)" , " 宅 zhai (house)" , " 安 an (safety)" , " 宫 gong (palace)", " 室 shi (room)" , " 宿 su (residence)" , " 寓 yu (residence)" , and " 宇 yu (eaves)". " 广 " indicates a wide house with a roof or a corridor without a wall, such as " 庙 miao (temple)" , " 府 fu (mansion)" , " 庭 ting (court)" , " 库 ku (warehouse)", " 廊 lang (corridor)" , and " 店 dian (store)" . These two categories of characters mostly refer to buildings with sharp or wide roofs. The characters with " 木 mu (wood)" as their form component are usually related to wood-structure buildings or the usage of wood components, such as " 楼 lou (building)" , " 柱 zhu (pillar)" , and " 梁 liang (girder)" . The characters referring to buildings and having " 土 tu (earth)" as their form component are generally related to earth and stone structures, such as " 墙 qiang (wall)" , " 城 cheng (city wall)" , and " 塔 ta (pagoda)" . These two categories also include many further characters.

Among numerous Han characters indicating buildings, the character "宫（閜）gong (palace)" is worthy of appreciation. It not only indicates a wide roof but also shows the features of planar layout. If we look at it directly we can see that the upper "宀" is the form of a wide roof and the two "口" below look like windows; but turn it ninety degrees and it looks like a building plan, with the two "口" indicating that there are many houses. The description of one character "宫" makes use of two observation angles to show the wide roof and planar layout of ancient architecture.

行

"行 xing (travel)" is a pictographic character. In Jiaguwen and Jinwen the characters of "行" looked like the common "cross" roads, so the character originally meant "big way" and "big road". Roads are there because people need to walk along them, so "行" also refers to walk. China is a vast country with mountains, rivers, lakes, forests, and deserts, and ancient people would often sigh and say "行 路 难 xinglunan (it is difficult to walk)". Short distances were accessible on foot, but major journeys required boats or carriages. The horse and carriage were the earliest means of transport, used to travel long distances. For example, during the Spring and Autumn Period (770–475BC) Confucius went to many princely states to spread his political opinions, travelling by cattle carts or horse-drawn carriages. After uniting China, Emperor Qinshihuang of the Qin Dynasty (221–206BC) visited many parts of his empire by means of horse-drawn chariots. Two such chariots, made of bronze, were unearthed from the mausoleum of Emperor Qinshihuang in Xi'an, and it is said that the Emperor used these conveyances to travel through his kingdom. "舟 zhou" means boat and is a pictographic character. In Jiaguwen, the character was quite clearly the representation of a small wooden boat. We can safely say that boat transport became significantly more developed in the Shang

Picture of Xuan Zang's Pilgrimage on Foot for Buddhist Scriptures.

Picture of Confucius Saint Deeds of Ming Dynasty (Part). It portrayed the scene that Confucius went to many princely states to spread his political opinions by cattle carts or horse-drawn carriages.

Dynasty (1600–1046 BC), and when Jian Zhen (688–763), a famous monk of the Tang Dynasty (618–907), crossed the eastern sea to preach Buddhism in Japan, and Zheng He (1371–1433), a Ming Dynasty Eunuch, visited South Asia, West Asia and Africa, they boarded very large ocean-going ships.

But some people did not take chariots or boats when making long journeys. The most famous is Xuan Zang (602–664), a monk of the Tang Dynasty (618–907). He set off from Xi'an to fetch the Buddhist classics from ancient India, and the folk tale The Pilgrim to the West was based on his experiences. The journey of Xuan Zang covered tens of thousands of miles, but it was accomplished on foot.

Kaishu

Jiaguwen

Jinwen

Xiaozhuan

Cultural Life

Cultural life in ancient times was extensive and colorful, so there are a large number of Han characters recording cultural life of the ancients. Introduced below are a few of important and commonly used Han characters.

乐

" 乐 yue (music)" is an associative-compound character. In Jiaguwen, the lower part of " 乐 " is a wood and the upper part is a string. The whole character resembles an ancient wooden stringed musical instrument. In Jinwen, something like the character " 白 " was added to the middle of the string, rather resembling the thumb plucking it. In fact, the original meaning of " 乐 " was stringed musical instrument. Later it became the general name for all musical instruments, and also refered to music. China is a country in which music is both constantly performed and very much appreciated. The ancient Shi Jing (Classics of Poetry) recorded more than 70 kinds of musical instruments, such as drum, fou (which is a uniquely Chinese traditional instrument), chime stone, bell, and various stringed instruments, and also many ancient pieces of music. Currently, the number of music scores of stringed musical instrument collected and kept in China has exceeded 3,000. In ancient times music was closely combined with dance and poetry. Every musical composition was accompanied by dance and many paintings, such as Picture of Singing and Dancing, have come down to us. We can thus share in some of those people's grand occasions of singing and dancing. Every poem was accompanied by singing, and the poems in the Shi Jing were all written to be sung, hence the noun " 诗歌 shige (poem and song)" in Chinese.

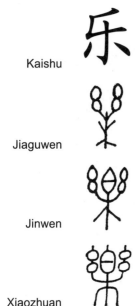

Kaishu

Jiaguwen

Jinwen

Xiaozhuan

The Musical Instruments in the Picture of a Night Banquet by Han Xizai. The picture described the scene that official Han Xizai of Southern Tang Dynasty of Five Dynasties and Ten Kingdoms Period held a night banquet to entertain the guests in the form of serial scroll.

Dancing in the Picture of Night Banquet by Han Xizai

Music can entertain people, so the meaning of " 乐 " was extended to cover joy and happiness, such as " 快乐 kuaile (enjoyment)" , " 欢乐 huanle (happy)" , and " 乐园 leyuan (land of pleasure)" . In these instances, though, the character " 乐 " is not pronounced as "yuè" but as "lè".

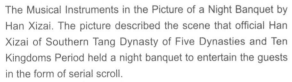

" 舞 wu (dance)" was originally a pictographic character. In Jiaguwen the character " 舞 " looked like somebody dancing, with a tree branch or ox tail in her hand, and originally meant dance. In Jinwen, two legs were added under the character and the image of the dancer became clearer. Also the character " 舞 " had become an associative-compound character. When

Kaishu

Jiaguwen

Jinwen

Xiaozhuan

dancing people would cry out " 呜 呜 (wuwu) !" and the pronunciation of the character " 舞 " , i.e. "wu" , might well have originated in this way. Our ancient forebears usually danced to express their emotions and wishes, especially when attempting to communicate with their ancestor gods, and hoped to receive a blessing from them. At that time there was always dancing as part of sacrificial or magical activities. On the famous "pottery basin painted with dancing patterns", dating back some 5,000 years and which was discovered in Qinghai Province, we can see the drawings of 15 dancing people on the inner surface. Five dancers comprised a group. They took steps in time to the beats and danced joyfully hand in hand, and the atmosphere was very intense. These members of primitive clans might be celebrating their success at hunting or participating in some form of wizardry. On the rock face of the Huashan Mountain there is a drawing of some grand occasion at which 1,900 persons danced together. The Huashan cliff painting is a record of several sacrificial activities for mountain and river gods. These red dancers take us right back to an ancient and mysterious world. In olden days, people would dance when worshipping dragons or praying for rain and favorable weather. We can certainly say that singing and dancing in these early times were not considered an amusement, but was an obligation connected with the day to day demands of laboring and living which, of course, was far more important.

Pottery Basin Painted with Dancing Patterns (Majiayao Culture). The picture vividly shows the hot scene that ancient people danced together in important events.

册

" 册 ce (book)", ancient book, is a pictographic character. Before the invention and use of paper, people had to carve characters on tortoise shells or animal bones or bronze ware, and these are what we know as Jiaguwen or Jinwen. People also wrote characters on strips of bamboo and bark, but these are comparatively thin and one leaf usually contained only one line of characters. If there were many characters, people had to bind together many bamboo and wooden strips using hemp or thread woven from cattle hide, and this was the " 册 ", i.e. " 简册 jiance (book made of slivers of wood or bamboo)". The ancient character " 册 " actually resembles such a book. Those vertical strokes painted one after another are the strips of bark, and the rounded horizontal stroke is the thread binding them together. Even today, in Kaishu the character " 册 " still looks like a book made in this way, but one that has been simplified to two strips of bamboo slips and one thread. As early as in the Jin Dynasty (265–420) many bamboo-slip books

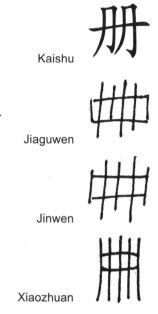

Kaishu

Jiaguwen

Jinwen

Xiaozhuan

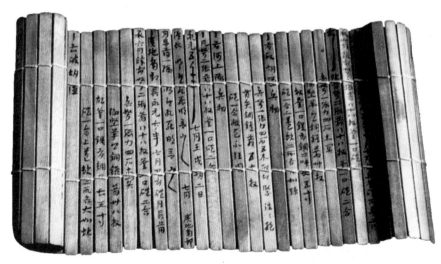

Wood-Strip Book of the Han Dynasty, unearthed from Juyan in Inner Mongolia

had been unearthed from the tombs of the Warring States Period (475–221 BC). The most famous is the Zhushu Jinian (Chronological Record on Bamboo Book). The book's name tells us that it is an historical work written on bamboo slips. Later, the buried bamboo and wood pages of the Qin (221–206 BC) and Han (206 BC –220 AD) Dynasties were constantly being unearthed in astonishing quantities. Just think about it: how heavy these ancient books must have been! It is said that Emperor Qinshihuang of the Qin Dynasty (221–206 BC) would read documents that weighed 60 kg! They even had to be carried to the imperial palace by strong-men. What he read were these books made of bamboo and wood bark. In China there is an idiom, " 学富五车 xuefu wuche" . It is used to indicate that a person is knowledgeable and has read many books, and originated in the Warring States Period (475–221 BC). It is said that at that time a man named Hui Shi was extremely knowledgeable and spent much time reading books. Every time he went out, he would be accompanied by five vehicles carrying his books. These books could only have been composed of strips of wood and bamboo.

Pursuit for Happiness and Luckiness

Chinese nation pursues happiness and luckiness, and people are always full of hope towards better life. Forms and structures of some Han characters reflect this kind of folk psychology, and such Han characters have become auspicious symbols loved very much by Chinese people.

福

" 福 fu (blessing)" is an associative-compound character. In Jiaguwen, " 福 fu (blessing)" is composed of " 礻 shi (sacrificial altar)" in the left and

" 酉 you (wine jar)" in the right, meaning sacrificial altar and wine jar respectively. The two components formed the meaning of using wine to sacrifice ancestors and gods to pray for blessings. One horizontal stroke in the " 酉 you (wine jar)" character indicates that the wine is full, but Xiaozhuan breaks the " 酉 you (wine jar)" into " 畐 fu", so the shape of a wine jar can not be seen anymore. Later, the meaning of " 酉 you (wine jar)" was extended from "full wine" to "fullness" and "perfect satisfaction", which is something pursued by Chinese throughout their lives.

Well then, what is " 福 fu (blessing)" exactly? There was a saying of "wufu (five blessings)" in ancient China, which is long life, richness, health, good morality, and peaceful life. It seems that it is not easy to enjoy all the five blessings. Actually, 福 fu (blessing) is "happiness" or "good fortune". The Chinese people always say "Peace is good fortune" and "No disaster and disease is good fortune", which are quite reasonable. In China, you will often not only hear people say but also see people write " 福 fu (blessing)"

Kaishu 福

Jiaguwen 福

Jinwen 福

Xiaozhuan 福

The character " 福 fu (blessing)" contains people's expectation of happiness and luck.

everywhere. During the Spring Festival, people paste " 福 fu (blessing)" onto doors, windows, or walls, believing that "fu" written on the red paper would bring good fortune and luckiness to the whole family. It is interesting that such "fu" characters are always pasted upside down. It is because that " 倒 dao (upside down)" and " 到 dao (arrive)" are the same in pronunciation. " 福倒了 ("fu" is upside down)" sounds like " 福到了 ("fu" has arrived)".

Figure of the God of Longevity

寿

" 寿 shou (life)" means a long life, which is desired by everyone. The complex font of " 寿 " is " 壽 ", whose original meaning is "prolonged life", which means a long life. There are many ways of writing " 寿 " in the Han characters. In Jiaguwen, it is a "s"-shaped symbol with two " 口 kou (mouth)" , pronounced as "chóu" . For more ancient characters, its upper part is " 老 lao (old)", indicating an old man who bent down and had little hair, and the lower part is the symbol pronounced chóu. Therefore, " 寿 " is a picto-phonetic character, pronounced chóu. In fact, the "s" symbol in the character in deed means a curved and long road. Therefore, it is better to treat " 寿 " as an associative-compounds character, indicating the tortuous and long life path of an old man. The "shou" character in Jinwen is more like an associative-compounds character. One hand and one " 口 kou (mouth)"are added to the lower part of such " 寿 ", and the entire character shows the sc-ene of raising a wine glass to congratulate an elderly person on his birthday. This hand (寸 cun) can still be found in simplified characters nowadays.

Kaishu

Jiaguwen

Jinwen

Xiaozhuan

There was a saying of "Superb lifetime of 100 years and medium lifetime of 80 years" in Chinese ancient books. Relatively grand birthday celebration activities are held on the 60, 70, 80 and 90 birthdays, and that day is called the " 寿日 shouri (birthday of an elderly person)" or " 寿辰

shouchen (birthday of an elderly person)". Chinese people often eat " 长寿面 chang shou mian (longevity noodles)" on their birthdays, which means the life is a long as the noodles. " 健康长寿 Jian kang chang shou (good health and a long life)" and " 寿比南山 shou bi nan shan (may you live as long as the Southern Mountain)" are often used to congratulate an elderly person on his birthday. In the folk auspicious drawings, there is an old man with a big forehead and fairly long mustache. He walks with the help of a walking stick and holds a peach in his hand, with smile on his faces all the time. It is the " 寿星 shou xing (the god of longevity)", or " 老人星 lao ren xing (the god of longevity)" or " 寿星老儿 shou xing lao er (the god of longevity)". Since ancient times, " 寿星 " has been the symbol of longevity, and all people like him.

和

Kaishu

Jiaguwen

Jinwen

Xiaozhuan

" 和 he" is a pictophonetic character. In Jiaguwen (inscriptions on bones or tortoise shells), " 和 " is already a pictophonetic character, which indicates that not all inscriptions on bones or tortoise shells are pictographic, and some characters already have phonographic components. The left part of " 和 he" in Jiaguwen is the component indicating meaning, which indicates the shape of " 笙 sheng (a kind of ancient Chinese wind instrument, made of several bamboo pipes) while the right part indicating sound is " 禾 he". " 和 he" in Jinwen is nearly the same as " 和 he" in Jiaguwen in terms of shape. " 和 he" in Xiaozhuan is almost the same as " 和 he" in Jiaguwen and Jinwen, but is more ordered. There is one noteworthy simplified shape in Xiaozhuan. The left part is " 口 kou (mouth)" while the right part is " 禾 he", from which Kaishu originated.

The original meaning of " 和 he" is the consonance and harmony of mu-

The Character " 和 he" in Beijing Olympic Games

sical sounds, and such extended meanings as gentleness, softness and peace developed later. "Harmony is the most precious" , the humanism idea of Confucius is a kind of expression of the "outlook on harmony" of Chinese nation. " 和 he (harmony)" is a very important feature of Chinese traditional culture. The core of Confucianism is " 仁 ren (benevolence)", which is actually the spirit of " 和 ". During the opening ceremony of the 2008 Beijing Olympic Games, a huge " 和 " appeared among the movable-type printing plates, representing Chinese people's advocacy and pursuit of " 和 ".

THE ART OF HAN CHARACTERS

Han characters are a kind of art. The art of Han characters is mainly represented by calligraphy, fine-art characters and the seals of Han characters. It has a particular charm unique among all the languages of all the nationalities of the world.

These characters originated from drawings. The square characters are the abstract representation of all the natural things around us, such as the sky, the earth, mountains and rivers, as well as an important insight into the thinking and creativity of the Chinese people. The pictrophatic elements of Han characters provide the art of Han characters with enough space of imagination and expression.

Calligraphic Art of Han Characters

Calligraphic art of Han characters is a unique line art capable for expressing emotions and manifesting artistic conceptions, making Han characters have a "life". The beauty and interest of Han characters are fully revealed by writers.

The Calligraphy of Ancient Character" 马 "by Han Meilin of Modern Time. This work vividly shows that "calligraphy and paintings have the same origin". From the aspect of the history of word, it can be said that "calligraphy and paintings have the same origin" (selected from Tianshu, Han Meilin) .

Line Art to Express Emotions

Put it shortly, Chinese calligraphy is an art of writing Han characters with writhing brushes. It is a kind of art expressing emotions by means of writing Han characters. Han characters' linear structure derived from drawings lays a solid foundation for calligraphy of Han characters. In ancient times, there was a saying that "calligraphy and paintings have the same origin", and it was believed that calligraphy and paintings are interlinked: both are expressed by lines and reflect the same natural world. Calligraphy is "drawing" characters and drawing is "writing" paintings. The beauty of Han calligraphy characters lies in the beauty of their lines. Han characters are composed of strokes that are represented by lines. Their form depends on the movement of lines and space to show various postures, motions, and meanings, so as to express different artistic conceptions, aesthetic perceptions, and emotions. Generally speaking, thick and heavy lines are powerful, thin and light lines are graceful; rounded and smooth lines make people feel happy, and the sere or pausal lines make people feel worried or distressed. As it were, Han characters calligraphy is a unique line art to express emotions. This kind of emotional expression with abstract lines is a striking feature differentiating the Chinese calligraphy from other forms of character writing. So that, Picasso, a Spanish drawing master, said that, "If I were born in China, I would certainly become a calligrapher instead of an oil painter".

Chinese Calligraphic Art Has a Long History

Some 3,000 years ago, when the people of the Shang Dynasty cut Jiaguwen characters on tortoise shells and animal bones with the point of a knife, the initial calligraphy creation had begun. Later, each dynasty achieved different degrees of chirographic style and nurtured countless excellent calligraphy works, such as Jinwen on bronze ware, Xiaozhuan on carving stones of the Qin Dynasty, Lishu on bamboo and wooden slips in the Han Dynasty, and Kaishu, Xingshu and Caoshu engraved on stone tablets or written on papers. Meanwhile, many outstanding calligraphers emerged, such as Li Si who was good at Xiaozhuan, "calligraphy master" Wang Xizhi, "four Kaishu masters" Yan Zhenqing, Liu Gongquan, Ouyang Xun and Zhao Mengfu, "Caoshu master" Zhang Xu. Generally speaking, Kaishu and Xingshu are the most important forms. For hundreds and thousands of years, people have adored Wang Xizhi of the Eastern Jin Dynasty (317–420) and Yan Zhenqing of the Tang Dynasty (618–907). The characters of Wang Xizhi are pretty and fluent while the characters of Yan Zhenqing are vigorous and majestic, and thus two schools came into being in calligraphy circles. Although these two schools have

Xingshu *Kuai Xue Shi Qing* Tie of Wang Xizhi. This was a letter, by which writer expressed his greetings to his relatives when the snow stopped. The work showed writer's relaxed and pleasant mood.

different styles, they both express thoughts and emotions through the art of calligraphy, demonstrating that calligraphy is an art reflecting writer's joy, anger, sorrow and happiness.

Wonderful Artistic Conception

Han characters originate from drawings. The pictographic elements in the square forms show the beauty of everything in the world. This is a visual beauty of shapes, and one that can inspire the imagination of artists and calligraphers. Phonetic words do not have these qualities. Since ancient times there have been many artistic works created by means of Han characters' pictographic elements. Some of these works have a very high level of artistic conception.

The character " 山 shan (mountain)" has a simple form with only three strokes. But under the pen of Mi Fu (1051–1107), a great calligrapher during the Song Dynasty (960–1279), it really looked like an ink painting of

Character " 山 shan (mountain)"
by Mi Fu

Landscape Painting by Mi Fu

Caoshu Character " 缚 fu (bind)" by Mao Zedong of modern time. The Calligrapher used the character " 缚 " to weave a dense and wide net and created an artistic conception.

high mountains. The three peaks rise up tall and straight, the thick strokes are very powerful, and anybody seeing it can appreciate the beauty of its conception. Mi Fu was also a great painter. He often painted mountains and had a deep feeling for them. It can be said that the character " 山 " represents the grand and majestic mountain in his mind. When writing the character " 山 ", it was as though he was using the brush pen to reveal his love for the mountain. In ancient times there was a saying that "calligraphy and paintings have the same origin", and it was believed that calligraphy and paintings are connected together and reflect the natural world. Calligraphy is "drawing" characters and drawing is "writing" paintings. Therefore, when we appreciate the calligraphy work of " 山 ", we feel as though we are admiring a Chinese landscape painting.

The pictographic elements of Han characters offered calligraphers plenty of scope for imagination and artistic representation. Let's have a look at the Caoshu " 缚 fu (bind)" by Mao Zedong (1893–1976), a modern calligrapher and poet. This character " 缚 " was written in one fluid action. It is vigorous and lively. The continuous strokes look like a big woven net. Depending on his artistic imagination, the calligrapher made full use of the form and meaning of the character " 缚 " and wrote it with a bold and generous spirit and beautiful calligraphic style. We can thoroughly appreciate the feeling of force and beauty.

Special Calligraphy Tool

Chinese calligraphy is a special art which uses a brush-pen. Whether appreciating or actually learning this art, you must have the correct tools for the job, and they are brush-pen, ink, ink stone and paper, which are affectionally known as the "four treasures in the study". These calligraphy tools decide the representational form, the effect and the features of the finished work. Without these basic tools, there would be no art of Chinese calligraphy, and without expertise in their use there would be no excellent calligraphy works.

"Four Treasures in the Study". The most famous "four treasures in the study" in China: brush-pen of Huzhou (produced in Huzhou, Zhejiang), ink of Huizhou (produced in Huizhou, Anhui), paper of Xuanzhou (produced in Xuanzhou, Anhui) and ink stone of Duanzhou (produced in Duanzhou, Guangdong).

Appreciation on Famous Calligraphy Treasures

Calligraphy of Han characters includes Jiaguwen, Jinwen, Xiaozhuan, Lishu, Kaishu, Xingshu and Caoshu etc. Therefore, we can learn about the artistic features of each chirography and the general development of calligraphy of Han characters, and experience the beauty and amusement of Han characters through appreciation on treasures of each chirography.

For Capturing Deer, a Treasure of Jiaguwen Calligraphy

Rubbings of For Capturing Deer Divination Carved in Cattle Bones (Shang Dynasty). It fully shows the feature of Jiaguwen that the strokes are thin, rigid, straight and protuberant.

Jiaguwen marked the beginning of Chinese calligraphic art and had showed a certain level of that, though it was an unconscious art.

It is a precious piece of cattle bone with engraved words which recorded the divination on a hunting activity of the Emperor of the Shang Dynasty (1600–1046 BC). The divination massage is that " 殻，贞：今日我其狩？狩获擒鹿五十又六 " which means: Qiao, zhen ren (name of an official position in the Shang Dynasty), divined and asked, "Will I (the Emperor of the Shang Dynasty) hunt smoothly today? " As a result, 56 deer were captured. It's surprising that 56 deer were captured only by one hunting activity. It indicates the large scale of hunting activity of the Emperor of the Shang Dynasty, the great number of wildlife and good ecological environment along the lower reach of the Yellow River in 3,000 years ago.

These characters in Jiaguwen were carved on cattle bone with the point of a knife, thus the strokes are thin, rigid, straight and protuberant, the curves are mostly square, and the characters are outstanding, which can be described as "the strokes are powerful enough to penetrate the medium", a jargon in the lips of calligraphers. In terms of structure, characters are mostly square, symmetric and harmonious despite of different sizes; in terms of layout, characters are arranged linearly in vertical direction but irregularly in horizontal direction, to show the beauty of scatter and mixture. The most wonderful place on the cattle bone is the pictographic character "者 (鹿)", which highlights the beautiful antler. The character is so simple and vivid as a whole that it totally seems a beautiful and unforgettable stick figure of animal.

Sanshi Plate Inscription, a Treasure of Jinwen Calligraphy

Jinwen on the bronze ware shows a simple beauty of calligraphy during the Shang (1600–1046 BC) and Zhou (1046–256 BC) Dynasties. Jinwen had appeared in the Shang Dynasty and reached its peak in the Western Zhou Dynasty (1046–771 BC).

The Sanshi Plate of the later period of the Western Zhou Dynasty was inscribed 357 characters on its underside and became the bronze ware with the second longest inscription in ancient times. The inscription recorded a land dispute between two princely states under the control of the Emperor of the Zhou Dynasty. The

Rubbings of Sanshi Plate Inscription (Late Western Zhou Dynasty). The style of Sanshi Plate Inscription is simple and vigorous.

characters in the inscription were inscribed in grotesquely skew and scattering forms and free, unconstrained, simple and vigorous strokes, and arranged linearly in vertical direction, irregularly in horizontal direction and closely as a whole. Jinwen were inscribed and thus the strokes are generous and mellow, totally varying from thin, rigid and straight Jiaguwen carved with the point of a knife. Calligraphic style of Jinwen can be categorized as the comely and mellow style and the simple and vigorous style. Sanshi Plate Inscription belongs to the latter that was popular among most calligraphers in various dynasties. Generally, many calligraphy lovers copy Sanshi Plate Inscription before learning Xiaozhuan calligraphy.

Yishan Carved Stone, a Treasure of Xiaozhuan Calligraphy

Having united China, Emperor Qinshihuang led a caravan of carts and horses and visited seven places, setting up a stone stele praising his merits at each of them. The inscriptions on these steles were written by Li Si in style of Xiaozhuan. *Yishan Carved Stone* was one of them.

Rubbings of Yishan Keshi (Stone Carving on the Yishan Mountain) (Part, Qin Dynasty). The beauty of rounded and curved strokes is the feature of Yishan Keshi.

Original *Yishan Carved Stone* had been destroyed before the Tang Dynasty, so this appreciated here is a copy engraved according to the rubbing of original stone inscription. Obviously, its layout is vertically and horizontally linear and in good order; the form and structure of characters are regular, symmetric, balanced and harmonious, and the upper part of character was close while the lower part was loose; and especially the strokes are rounded and curved, fluent and consistently thick to show the beauty of

curves. Generally, we see calligraphy works of Xiaozhuan with those characteristics. Although it was replaced by Lishu soon, the forms and lines of Xiaozhuan have been popular among calligraphy lovers in later generations, and up to now Xiaozhuan is still applied to calligraphy works and seals by calligraphers.

Stele of Sacrificial Vessels, a Treasure of Lishu Calligraphy

Rubbings of *Stele of Sacrificial Vessels* (Part, Eastern Han Dynasty). The style of *Stele of Sacrificial Vessels* is steady and elegant.

Lishu calligraphy reached its peak through inscriptions on steles in the Eastern Han Dynasty (25–220). These works are in diverse styles e.g. some are simple and sturdy; some solemn but deeply attractive; some steady and elegant; and some unrestrained with various forms. *Stele of Sacrificial Vessels* is a representative excellent work in solemn but deeply attractive calligraphy style, and recorded events of the decoration of Confucius Temple in Qufu and the fabrication of sacrificial vessels. The forms of characters are oblong; the structures are tight; the waves of strokes are obvious; and the strokes extending outward let characters full of grandeur. Especially, the strokes are thin, rigid and vigorous while strokes rising upward are thick and heavy, showing the beauty of vigor and rhythm of the whole work. *Stele of Sacrificial Vessels* has had great impacts on works later in terms of artistic features e.g. its direct influence over *Stele of Preface of Holy Doctrine* at the foot of Dayan Tower, a famous Kaishu work in the Tang Dynasty. Many calligraphers in the Qing Dynasty loved *Stele of Sacrificial Vessels* very much and praised it as "No.1 Stele of the Han Dynasty".

Rubbings of *Yan Qinli Stele* (Part, Yan Zhenqing of Tang Dynasty). *Yan Qinli Stele* embodies the beauty of generosity and majesty.

Yan Qinli Stele, a Treasure of Kaishu Calligraphy

Kaishu is the most typical chirography of Chinese calligraphy. Kaishu calligraphy had been achieved a lot in the Tang Dynasty where Ouyang Xun, Yan Zhenqing, Liu Gongquan and other famous Kaishu calligraphers started to appear. Yan Zhenqing created a magnificent chirography which has square characters and thick and heavy strokes and was called "Yan Style" later. "Yan Style" shows a generous and elegant beauty and is common and easy to learn after absorbing features that ordinary people transcribed Han characters. And it became the chirography with largest impact on Chinese calligraphic art for thousands of years.

Yan Qinli Stele is the representative work in Yan Zhenqing's later years and can embody his majestic and solemn Kaishu style most. Its characters are square and full, as if filling the panes, and thus seem majestic but not clumsy. The horizontal strokes are thin while dot, vertical, left-falling and right-falling are thick, showing a very obvious comparison of thickness. Square characters have rounded strokes while straight lines mix with curves, showing the beauty of power as if every character can extend outward. It is better to say works in Yan Zhenqing's later years embody the beauty of generosity and majesty rather than comeliness and morbidezza. It is a completely different beauty filled with power, which is the typical style of "Yan Style" . *Yan Qinli Stele* is an outstanding Kaishu work of Yan Zhenqing and the best model of calligraphy to learn Kaishu.

Lan Ting Xu, a Treasure of Xingshu Calligraphy

Wang Xizhi, a great calligrapher in the Eastern Jin Dynasty (317–420), was honored as "the master of calligraphy" in ancient China. *Lan Ting Xu* in Xingshu is the most famous one among Wang Xizhi's calligraphy works in various chirographies and was honored as "No.1 running-hand work of all over the world".

In the spring of the ninth year of Yonghe, Eastern Jin Dynasty (353 AD), Wang Xizhi with his friends had a party in Lan Ting where everyone was drinking, writing poems and collecting them into an anthology. At that time, Wang Xizhi wrote an extemporaneous preface for the poetry anthology — *Lan Ting Xu*. There are 28 lines and 324 characters in *Lan Ting Xu*. It is an enjoyment to appreciate *Lan Ting Xu*. Opening the volume, familiar Xingshu characters come into sight vigorously, gracefully and fluently, and give out the happy romantic charm and the excited emotion of the writer. The whole preface is fluent with continual meaning, and the thin and thick strokes form the thickness of characters, to show a flowing beauty and a natural and peaceful artistic conception. Wherein, every character is

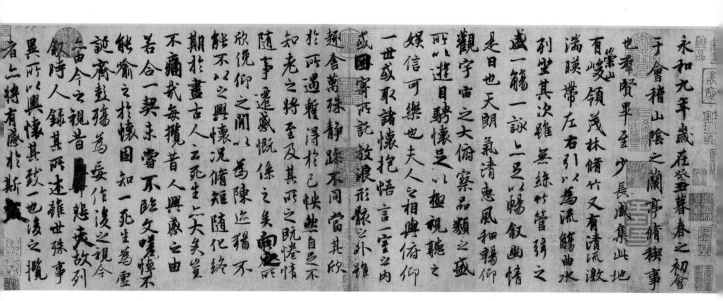

Xingshu *Lan Ting Xu* (Part, Wang Xizhi of Eastern Jin)

outstanding even the same character has different changes. For example, there are 20 " 之 (zhi)" in the whole preface which all vary in forms and styles of writing. It is said that Wang Xizhi himself also liked the work very much, and wrote it for more another 100 times after the party but those all could not compare with the original work.

Lan Ting Xu appreciated currently was transcribed by calligrapher in the Tang Dynasty. It is said that the original work was buried in his mausoleum as the burial object by Li Shimin, the Emperor of the Tang Dynasty who loved Wang Xizhi's calligraphy.

Four Ancient Poems, a Treasure of Caoshu Calligraphy

Zhang Xu was a famous Caoshu calligrapher of the Tang Dynasty, and *Four Ancient Poems* is his representative and only extant authentic Kuangcao work and has become the national treasure of China. People admire Zhang Xu's cursive-hand works very much and called him "the master of cursive hand".

There are four poems in Ancient Four Poems. It is an artistic feast to appreciate the work. These lively and vigorous characters were connected their strokes together fluently and naturally and finished once, showing a great majesty. The changes in forms of characters are also very wonderful. Sometimes two characters seem to be one while one character seems to be two at another time, therefore it is difficult for people who are ignorant of Caoshu to tell these characters apart. Kuangcao is an art for calligraphers to release their passion. It is said that Zhang Xu liked drinking very much, and each time he was drunk, he would write Caoshu while shouting. Sometimes he would use his hairs to write before picking up a writhing brush, so that he himself could not know how he wrote those unrestrained characters on papers after sobering up. Kuangcao is a pure calligraphic art which has lost

the practicability of Han characters, just pursues the beauty of lines and the expression of emotions, and brings an extremely high artistic appreciation to people.

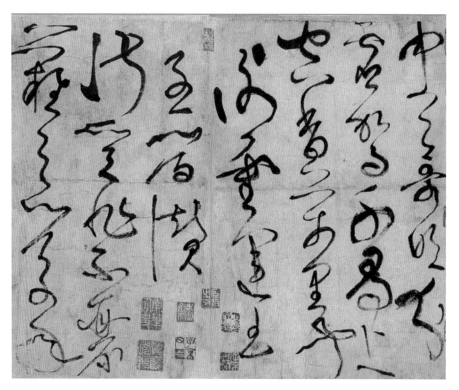

Cursive Hand *Four Ancient Poems* by Zhang Xu of the Tang Dynasty. The strokes are powerful, while the lines are vivid. Even if you don't completely understand the characters, you will still recognize their beauty. That is the charm of calligraphy.

Commercial-art Han Characters

Commercial-art characters have an artistic design. They reflect the visual beauty and decorative effects of characters, and pictographic characters paved the way for the creation of commercial-art characters.

Beautiful Foreign Fine-art Characters

Commercial-art Han characters have an artistic design and serve the function of beautifying things. The upper and lower case printed characters in newspaper, magazines, and books, and the variety of typeface characters on advertisements, handbills, posters, and packaging are all commercial-art characters, exquisitely designed by artists. Commercial-art Han characters are different from calligraphy, but both represent the art of Han characters. Calligraphy reflects the beauty of pen and ink and the writer's thoughts and feelings, while the commercial-art characters reflect the beauty of design of Han characters with the addition of some decorative effects. Commercial-art Han characters are different from comparable foreign words. The latter are still based on the Roman alphabet but they do not have a pictographic element. But Han characters do have such an element, and their colorful strokes and forms cannot be duplicated by another writing system.

On the basis of the Roman alphabet, the foreign commercial-art words are, after decorative elaboration, also beautiful, but this alphabet is limited to the small number of comparatively simple forms. But Han characters, on the basis of their being pictographic, are more colorful with regard to strokes and forms, so they more easily lend themselves to decorative effects.

Ancient Public-art Characters

Since the birth of Han characters, there have appeared public-art versions. Such a style, with its decorative effects, has always played an important role in beautifying day to day items. Examples of ancient public-art characters mainly include totems, clan badges, bird and insect calligraphy, Xiaozhuan and characters in the style of the Song Dynasty (960–1279).

The Earliest Public-art Characters in Ancient Times

Clan Badges and Totem Characters. The clan badges and totem characters on the bronze ware of the Shang (1600–1046 BC)and Zhou Dynasties (1046–221 BC)were the earliest public-art characters subsequent to the Chinese written language reaching maturity, and were popular for more than 500 years. The decorative style and primitive simplicity represented by such characters had a great influence over the characters and decorative art of later generations.

The Strangest Public-art Characters in Ancient Times

Bird and Insect Calligraphy. During the Spring and Autumn Period (770–475 BC) and Warring States Period (475–221 BC), a form of characters decorated with birds, insects, animals and fish started to appear on the bronze ware of all the princely states — bird and insect calligraphy. These characters have extended forms and curved lines, and are lively and vivid. They are rather strange, but fascinating. As fine-art characters, these

Graphic Character " 龙 龍 long (dragon)" on Bronze Ware. This drawing-character " 龙 long (dragon)" carved on items of bronze ware depicts the image of a dragon. It is vivid, simple and symmetrical, and is nothing less than an exquisite drawing of a dragon.

Inscription of Character " 鹿 lu (deer)" on Bronze Ware

bird and insect images are well-developed compared to the totem characters on the bronze wares of the Shang and Zhou Dynasties. The beautiful style of the calligraphy reflected the aesthetic interests and positive feelings of the people at that time. Bird and insect calligraphy reflected people's love of nature and were popular for more than 300 years. After the Spring and Autumn Period and Warring States Period, they gradually disappeared.

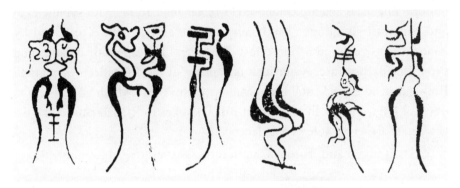

Beautiful Bird and Insect Calligraphy (the Spring and Autumn Period and Warring States Period. The six characters carved in bronze ware in bird and insect calligraphy are" 王 wang 子 zi 于 yu 之 zhi 用 yong 戈 ge".

The Most Beautiful Fine-art Characters in Ancient Times

Xiaozhuan. In various styles of Han characters, Zhuanshu, referring to Xiaozhuan of the Qin and Han Dynasties, have the strongest pictorial quality. During the Qin (221–206 BC) and Han (206 BC–220 AD) Dynasties, very decorative Xiaozhuan characters were often inscribed on stone steles, eave-tiles, weapons, seals, and bronze coins. Xiaozhuan have rounded and beautiful strokes, symmetrical forms, wonderfully decorative features and can quite rightly be considered as a kind of fine-art characters. In particular, Xiaozhuan in the Han Dynasty (206 BC–220 AD) had a wide

scale and the strokes and forms were colorful and attained the brilliant peak of Zhuanshu fine-art characters. Today Zhuanshu are still much admired, and many Chinese people are accustomed to cutting name seals in Xiaozhuan. You can see such beautiful characters on calligraphic scrolls, traditional Chinese paintings, advertisements, newspapers and magazines, buildings, dresses, electric appliances, stamps, and the national currency.

The basic strokes of Xiaozhuan are vertical, curved and horizontal, with uniform thickness and are composed of rectangular forms with symmetrical and balanced structures. The beauty of line and structure reflected by Xiaozhuan is required of the finest characters. In respect of balance and symmetry of structure, Xiaozhuan is capable of the fullest representation. Both independent and combined characters, plus those which go from up to down or left to right, can have symmetrical strokes in Xiaozhuan, so that the characters are as a whole very balanced.

Eaves Tile (the Han Dynasty). The four characters carved in eaves tile are " 汉 han 并 bing 天 tian 下 xia". The strokes are round and extended, which shows the beauty of curved line of calligraphy.

Collected Annotation of the Analects of Confucius, Carved Copy of Yuan Dynasty. The horizontal strokes are flat and thin, and the vertical strokes are straight and thick; the ending of a horizontal stroke has a triangular flourish, and the turning of a stroke has a square decoration. It shows that Songtizi character has become mature in Yuan Dynasty.

The Most Important Fine-art Characters in Ancient Times

Songtizi Characters. After the invention of engraving and wood printing in Sui Dynasty (581–618) and Tang Dynasty (618–907), people began to use knives to engrave early books. For rapid engraving, a set of square characters with flat and thin horizontal strokes and straight and thick vertical strokes became popular, i.e. the songtizi (characters with the style of the Song Dynasty (960–1279)). Songtizi characters are an improvement on the strokes and structures of Kaishu and became a fixed style that was convenient for engraving and also maintained a decorative quality. We refer to them as songti fine-art characters. It became perfected during the Ming (1368–1644) and Qing (1616–1911) Dynasties and is the genesis of the finest modern art-characters.

Songtizi characters continued to exert a great influence over later generations and remain widely used. Modern printing presses mainly adopt this form. Meanwhile, it is the basis of various finely drawn characters, so songtizi characters are still very important.

The features of songtizi characters are these: the horizontal strokes are flat and thin, and the vertical strokes are straight and thick; the ending of a horizontal stroke has a triangular flourish, and the turning of a stroke has a square decoration (these decorations are natural result of engraving with reduced cuttings); all the characters, no matter how many strokes they have, must fill identically sized panes. The beauty of songtizi characters ultimately resides in their neatness.

Modern Han Fine-Art Characters

Modern commercial-art characters were developed from songtizi. As an art form they are represented by the printing and hand-painting of fine characters. The major types are songti and boldface, along with various other styles of characters.

Songti Fine-art Characters

Songtizi characters are the basis of various fine-art characters. They are neat, beautiful, lively and visually appealing. They can be square, oblong and rectangular. The flat and thin horizontal strokes and straight and thick vertical strokes, plus elaborations of these strokes are its major features. It has a wide usage. We commonly see it in books, newspapers and magazines.

Among these songti characters, there is a kind which imitates the songtizi. It has longer forms, strokes with even thickness, horizontal strokes inclining upwards to the right, and is visually very attractive. Imitation songti characters are the prettiest and the most elegant, and are often used to write notation, explanatory notes, sub-titles, exhibition plates, and poems.

Boldface Characters

Boldface fine-art characters were also developed from songtizi characters. They thicken

宋体美术字

Printed Song-Dynasty Style Fine-art Characters. The horizontal strokes are thin and the vertical strokes are thick and strongly embellished. They appear to us as being neat, natural, lively and beautiful.

黑体美术字

Printed Boldface Fine-Art Characters. Boldface characters have square and concise forms and broad strokes. The horizontal and vertical strokes have the same thickness, and they omit any decorative flourishes. They look simple, natural, weighty and powerful, and are visually striking.

数风流人物，还看今朝。
只识弯弓射大雕。俱往矣，
风骚。一代天骄，成吉思汗，
略输文采，唐宗宋祖稍逊
英雄竞折腰。惜秦皇汉武，
江山如此多娇，引无数
看红装素裹，分外妖娆。
欲与天公试比高。须晴日，
滔。山舞银蛇，原驰蜡象，
余莽莽，大河上下，顿失
万里雪飘。望长城内外，惟
北国风光，千里冰封，
沁园春 雪
一九三六年二月
阔笔长仿宋

Hand-written Imitation Song-Dynasty Style Fine-Art Characters Made by Pen. These attractive and elegant imitation Song-Dynasty characters add a unique quality to this passage of handwritten poetry.

the horizontal strokes of these characters so that the horizontal and vertical strokes have the same thickness, and they omit any decorative flourishes. Boldface characters have square and concise forms and broad strokes, and look simple, natural, weighty and powerful, and are visually striking. Boldface characters are easy to write and have a wide application. They are often used for headlines, slogans, book titles, and advertisements. The colorful modern versions are mostly formed by the processing of boldface characters.

Variant Fine-Art Characters

Variant fine-art characters exhibit changes to the style of songtizi and boldface characters. Due to their symmetrical structure, concise form and decorative convenience, many boldface characters have been converted to this style. Variant fine-art characters are vivid, lively, interesting and full

" 虎 hu (tiger)" (Decoration on Stamp). The Jiaguwen character of " 虎 hu (tiger)" was changed to a beautiful fine-art character, in which the ancient pictographic character shines out of the modern version.

of artistic inspiration. They have a considerably wide usage and are very popular.

Variant fine-art characters have a number of forms and many of these are directly based on songtizi and boldface characters. For example, the Youyuan fine-art style has altered the two ends and turns of the strokes of boldface characters into rounded forms, while Changmei boldface is the combination of songtizi and boldface characters, and there are also several other styles with altered strokes.

Among the variant fine-art characters, there is a kind which exhibits a strongly pictorial quality, and these are called variant picture fine-art characters. They make full use of the pictographic elements and inventiveness of shape of Han characters, the designs and images are both vivid and interesting, and they emphasize the particular charm of pictographic characters. These are the most favored variant fine-art characters.

Hand-Written Variant Fine-Art Character " 术 shu (Art)". It is quite plain to see that these variant fine-art characters with different forms have all been changed from boldface characters.

Seal Art of Han Characters

Many foreign students studying here in China are given Chinese name seals after mastering the language. It is not uncommon to see them proudly showing these carved stones to their friends and classmates, explaining the curving characters, and unable to hide their pride and joy at possessing a such a precious treasure-they know once their names are carved on these small stones, the stones attain life and soul.

Seal Art

Carved seals of Han characters are also called made seals. As they are mostly composed of Zhuan characters, they are also known as Zhuanke (seal cutting). People use a knife to cut the Han characters on jade, ivory, animal horn, wood, copper, gold and silver, and it is a process with a particular artistic style. Beginning in ancient times, these seals were widely used as a warrant.

Printed Characters on "Lute"

Back in the days of the Qin (221–206 BC) and Han (206 BC–220 AD) Dynasties there was no paper and all the documents and letters had to be written on strips of bamboo and wood. Before being delivered, in order to prevent any unauthorized reading or tampering the official would thoroughly bind the bamboo or wooden pages with thread, then seal its knot with a piece of clay, impressing it with an emblem representing the imperial government or the individual author. After it dried out the clay became very hard, and the three-dimensional impression upon its surface was "lute". If the lute was broken, it was obvious that some person had opened the document. It can be said that these seals were warrants to authorize inspection of the contents. Archaeologists have discovered that the seals for lute were almost all "white-character" seals (see the following passage). The characters on the seals were concave, and after the seals were pressed on the lute, the characters on the lute were raised. Later, there appeared silk and paper, so people no longer used the lute, directly pressing the seals onto the paper or silk. The emergence of lute promoted the development of seals.

Official and Private Seals

The ancient Chinese seals can, on the whole, be divided into official and private seals. Official seals were the symbol of position and power and were cut by emperors or government officials. Private seals were the name seals of ordinary people and were more colorful and had more lively forms than the official ones. In ancient times, these private seals were called " 印 yin" , " 印信 yinxin" , " 印章 yinzhang" and " 图章 tuzhang" , and the seals of emperors were " 玺 xi" or " 宝 bao".

Rubbings of the Seal of Prince Chengyang, a Lute of the Qin Dynasty

Material Object of Qitie Official Seal, a Lute of the Han Dynasty

Gold Seal of "King Weinu of the Han Dynasty" (the Eastern Han Dynasty)

Gold Seal, the "Seal of the Emperor" of the Qing Dynasty

Seals of the Literary Scholars

Jade, copper, gold and silver are very hard and thus difficult to make into seals. At first the seals of painters and calligraphers were specially made by professional seal cutters. During the Yuan (1206–1368) and Ming (1368–1644) Dynasties, some painters and calligraphers discovered types of stone that were comparatively soft and easy to carve. Then they started to use a knife and personally cut their own seals. They regarded knives as just another kind of pens and brought their artistic abilities into full play on these small stones. Thereafter, seals fully entered the realms of art. After completing works of calligraphy or painting, the artists would

When collecting books and calligraphy and painting works, Chinese people liked to print their own seals on them to demonstrate their ownership. This famous ancient painting Zhao Ye Bai by Han Gan, a painter of the Tang Dynasty, is covered all over with the seals of previous collectors.

press their personal seals onto them to indicate that they were their works and expressed their own thoughts, emotions and artistic interests. All works of calligraphy and painting were signed in this way. Of these, the traditional Chinese paintings are most especially the combination of "poetry, calligraphy, painting and seal". It is believed that a traditional Chinese painting without a seal is not a complete work, and the small red seal plays an important role in beautifying and balancing the painting.

Beauty of Seals

There are usually two ways of cutting seals; white-character and red-character. White-character (commonly known "intaglio character") seals are directly cut onto the stone and after being pressed onto a red inkpad the resulting characters are white and background is red. Red-character (usually referred to as "relief character") seals are cut around the strokes of the characters, leaving them raised, and when printed they are red.

The beauty of seals is displayed in their exquisite calligraphy, skill in cutting, and arrangement, such as the beautiful representations of Zhuanshu,

White-Character Seal *Yu Yan Lou* (玉砚楼) by Huang Yi of the Qing Dynasty

Red-character Seal *Jiangnan Buyi* (江南布衣) by Qi Baishi of Modern Time

Kaishu and Lishu, the various skills and artistry of manipulating the knife, and the artful arrangement of characters in a small space. One error in any of these aspects will ruin the whole work. In the art of seal-cutting, its soul is mainly represented by the maker's skill with the knife. We judge the level of seal art by the visual effect of these knife cutting skills. Those works which exhibit the greatest degree of skillful cutting are most prized. For example, the red-character seal " 江南布衣 Jiangnan Buyi" by Qi Baishi (1864–1957), a great modern painter, is both simple and exquisite. The four Zhuanshu characters are inserted into each other and are dependant on each other. They compose, with beautiful artistry, a square form. The cut strokes are thick or thin, continuous or separated. It seems that they were finished within the space of a single breath-a fine example of the art of skillful cutting.

Image Seals

Among the various types of seals there is one kind known as "image seals" . They are cut with the images of animals and people. Such drawing-seals were first printed on the lute of bamboo and wooden strips as symbols

Image Seal Deer (the Warring States Period)

Image Seal Hunting Tiger (the Han Dynasty)

Chinese Seal·Dancing Beijing (Modern Time)

or expressions of the maker's interests. Later, they developed into exquisite artworks which anybody could appreciate. Image seals appeared very early, and became more widely prevalent during the Spring and Autumn Period (770–475 BC) and Warring States Period (475–221 BC). People of the Han Dynasty (206 BC–220 AD) liked image seals very much. There were many examples with colorful content and simple and interesting forms, combined with a deep spirit. After the Han Dynasty (206 BC–220 AD), however, image seals fell out of favor. Nevertheless, they exhibit a beauty of design and continue to have a very high appreciation value. In modern times they have become popular again, and there have appeared many excellent works. The badge of the 2008 Olympic Games in Beijing, "Chinese Seal·Dancing Beijing", adopts the form of an image seal.

Appreciation of Exquisite Seal Art

For thousands of years, calligraphers, painters and seal cutting enthusiasts have made many seals in their own particular styles. The following exquisite works we have chosen to present to you are just a

" 文彭之印 Wen Peng's Seal" by Wen Peng of the Ming Dynasty

"柴门深处 Chaimen Shenchu (Deep Place from the Gate of Wood)" by He Zhen of the Ming Dynasty

" 敬 身 Jing Shen " by Ding Jing of the Qing Dynasty

" 伯 寅 藏 书 Boyin Cangshu (Book Preserved by Boyin)" by Zhao Zhiqian of the Qing Dynasty

" 梅 花 无 尽 藏 Meihua Wujin Cang (Preserved by Meihua Wujin)" by Wu Changshuo of the Qing Dynasty

" 白石 Baishi" by Qi Baishi of Modern Time

fraction of all the wonderful examples that have come down to us since the Ming (1368–1644) and Qing (1616–1911) Dynasties.

Calligraphy, fine-art characters and seals represent the high point of Han character art, and are also a precious cultural heritage of the Chinese people. Today, Han character art is still developing and new and excellent works with original styles and methods of representation are constantly appearing. We can safely say that Han character art will continue to add brilliance and color to the Chinese culture.

STEPPING INTO INFORMATION AGE

With information age coming in 1970s, ancient Han characters confronted an unprecedented challenge: China would be excluded from the information world if the Han characters had not been able to be typed into electronic computers like alphabetic writing. For thousands of years, the fate of Han characters has never been so closely linked with a technology.

Computer Processing of Han Character Information

Surprisingly, Han characters not only successfully integrated into today's information tide, but also exhibited an extraordinarily outstanding performance, from which we can not but marvel at the quality of the Han character itself.

During first half of the 20th century, with the introduction of western advanced cultures into China, it was believed that China fell behind owing to Han characters and thus alphabetic writing was recommended to replace them. Fortunately, Han characters dispelled those people's worries and steadily moved forward with their own strengths. However, with the rapid development of computer science all over the world during second half of the 20th century, some people again argued that Han characters will hinder the development of science due to the square characters could not be input into computers and further asserted that "the computer would be the gravedigger of square Han characters." But the fact dispelled those people's prejudice and pessimistic argument and the Han characters have narrowly passed through that crisis once again.

Successful Input of Han Characters into Computers

Because the electronic computer was invented by Westerners to deal with alphabetic writing whose words can be structured by a small number of letters through different linear arrangements, information input is the first conundrum to be solved for the computer processing of Han character information. For example, there are only 26 letters for English, plus numbers, punctuations and symbols etc., it's enough to set 50-60 basic keys on the keyboard. Then just by setting the relationships between those keys and binary codes, all source programs compiled with English letters can be changed into machine languages or any file in English can be input into machine for processing. However, it's much more difficult for computer to deal with Han characters, since square Han characters have such a great number of independent plane morphological symbols with complex structures and features such as polyphone vs. several characters with the same sound, and polysemous character vs. several characters with the same meaning. There are 60,000 Han characters whose basic strokes are not too many but can constitute various "components" with different meaning when the same stroke is put at different positions. As a result, it's required to set a big keyboard with 600 keys for more than 600 meaningful components, which is obviously impracticable.

How to do it? The only approach is converting Han character to western language or numbers, which are then changed into machine language. This means that Han character information processing must go through the "coding" process. It makes people remind of the very useful "telegraph codes" for Han characters invented over 100 years ago, where a Han character is represented by four numbers together. But telegraph codes are not related to voice and strokes. They require learning by rote and are extremely low efficient. Having found the direction, many researchers started making breakthroughs. First, they took apart the forms of Han characters and coded

them, that is, "glyph code" . Since 1970s, there were "code of radicals", "triangle code" , "code of strokes and letters" and "5-stroke code" and other glyph codes successively. The rapid speed is the advantage of glyph code. Another is the "phonetic code" that uses alphabetic writing to code. Scheme of the Chinese Phonetic Alphabet lays foundation for research on phonetic code. Every Han character has regulated pronunciation, thus phonetic codes such as "full spelling" , "binary syllabification", "simplified spelling" and "intelligent binary syllabification" are developed successively and successfully after continual explorations. The phonetic codes have become the first choice for most Chinese today thanks to its simpleness and ease to learn. There is also a kind of "phonetic & glyph code" using a combination of pronunciation and form to code characters with its own features. In recent years, there are non-keyboard input methods including the voice input and tablet input, which provide a new way to process Han character information. At present there are nearly one thousand Han character input methods, among which the speed of some input methods is not inferior to that of alphabetic writing. It is reported that inputting an essay in Han characters is faster than that in English.

The Advent of Laser Phototypesetting Technology for Han Characters

In 1970s, a number of western books and newspapers have been printed by "electronic phototypesetting technology" , a new technology that utilized computers to control and achieve phototypesetting and could be used for type setting and outputting of texts and images. The technology can be regarded as a revolution in printing history due to the high speed and delicacy it brought in printing and publishing industry. However, China was still in the movable type printing era with "lead and fire" at that time. Movable type printing was initially invented by Bi Sheng (about 970–1051) of Song Dynasty and used clay movable type at that time. After being introduced to Europe, German Gutenberg invented lead movable type printing according to its principle in the 15th century. Lead movable type printing requires manually picking and spelling the words one by one, which costs time, labor and resources and will also cause lead pollution.

How to achieve typesetting of Han characters by computers? The first thing would be to store Han character information into computers. But the amount of Han character information is too large while Chinese-made computer memory was only 64K at that time. Wang Xuan, a Peking University professor specialized in mathematics, took great interest in electronic phototypesetting technology and devoted himself to researching strokes of Han characters. He used a mathematical method of outline plus parameters to reduce the large Han character information by 500 times,

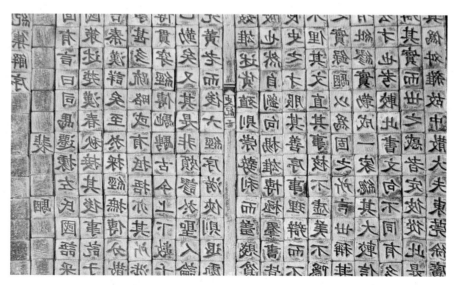

Movable Type Printing Invented by Bi Sheng (Model)

Modern Bi Sheng – Wang Xuan

cleaning the biggest barrier for development work. Having worked hard for over 10 years, overcame various difficulties and skipped the popular 2nd and 3rd phototypesetters in Japan, Europe and America, Wang Xuan and his team directly developed the 4th-generation laser phototypesetter, making Chinese publishing and printing industry "say goodbye to lead and fire and welcome light and electricity" since then and enter into the most advanced laser phototypesetting field from behindhand letter typesetting in one step. It takes 4 hours to typeset a piece of Chinese newspaper by letter typesetting while only 20 minutes by laser phototypesetting and the characters and figures are clear and bright in color. The laser phototypesetting technology developed by Wang Xuan has been applied widely and occupied 99% market shares of newspaper industry in China and 80% of Chinese newspaper industry in foreign countries in no time. Wang Xuan was honored as "Modern Bi Sheng".

Cheers and Worries in the Information Age for Han Characters

With gradual popularization of computers, Chinese find that there are less and less opportunities to write with pens while "forget the word with the pen in hand" happens frequently. When many people cannot write the word " 尴尬 " (gan ga, means "embarrassment"), Chinese writing ability for Han characters is confronting unprecedented embarrassment.

Rapid Degradation of Writing Ability for Han Characters

With the appearance and popularization of computers, it becomes very easy and rapid to write Han characters only with keyboard and mouse; the vast multitude of Chinese classics can also be stored in digital libraries. A wide spread never seen before happens to Han character culture due to computer science, showing a new surprising prosperity brought by information age.

Forget the Word with the Pen in Hand

However, on the other hand, there are many Han characters cannot be written out because the people are rarely using pens to write words for a long time, causing it becomes very common for the people to "forget the word with pen in hand" or wrongly write characters. Not to speak for characters with more strokes such as " 尴尬 (gan ga), 喷嚏 (pen ti), 饕餮 (tao tie), 邋遢 (la ta), 羸弱 (lei ruo), 盥洗 (guan xi)" which are hard to be

written, some people even can't write the common words with less strokes such as " 钥匙 (yao shi), 扫帚 (sao zhou), 纽扣 (niu kou), 拐弯 (guai wan), 视频 (shi pin), 厉害 (li hai), 针灸 (zhen jiu), 牙膏 (ya gao), 辣椒 (la jiao), 疑问 (yi wen)". No wonder someone joked that people have had "character amnesia" . Additionally, students tend to write at a decreasing level of standard and appearance as a whole. Their written characters have many wrong places and are illegible and ugly. The replacement of pens by keyboard and mouse rapidly decreases people's basic ability to write Han characters when bringing convenience. Indeed, it is a so severe fact at present that some people exclaim that Han characters go far away and become our "familiar strangers" in the keyboard age.

We shall inherit and pass down Han characters as the excellent cultural heritage of Chinese nation. Now it is more important that the whole society shall attach importance to handwriting Han characters and let people enhance the ability to write characters well. Writing is a basic skill, thus it is unpractical to think writing unnecessary from now on in the information age. The recent TV programs such as Chinese Dictation Congress of Chinese Characters and Hero of Chinese Characters are to call for the whole society to write Han characters and improve the awareness of passing down and protecting Han characters. In the competitions, primary and secondary school students showed a high-level ability to dictate and write Han characters, making the occasion warm and entertaining and arousing people's interest in and pursuit of handwriting Han characters again.

Network Language Needs To Be Standardized

In recent years, there are many weird characters on network such as "炗, 烎, 啚, 夒 and 曇 " which are popular among young people, are used by a small circle of persons and unknown to most people. Although some characters are interesting, e.g. " 癋 " looks like someone falling into water and means "drowning" while " 吅 " looks like 4 big open mouths and means "yelling" , these characters shall not be used again because they are variant Han characters abolished long age, or self-created characters belonging to non-standard characters.

Meanwhile, many network languages mainly for laugh and recreation are popular among young people now. Wherein, some characters are derived from dialects e.g. " 给力 " (gei li) is a northern dialect derived from " 乏力 " (fa li), but now means wonderful and great. When appearing on network for the first time, the word " 给力 " (gei li) became popular among netizen immediately and now is widely applied. Such new network languages are very vigorous and enrich vocabulary of Han characters. In addition, " 伊妹

After the programs including Hero of Chinese Characters become popular, there is an upsurge of "writing Han characters by hand". The photo shows that a primary school is holding a Han character dictation competition.

儿 " (yi mei er, means e-mail), " 驴友 " (lv you, means travel companion), " 菜鸟 " (cai niao, means green hand), " 杯具 " (bei ju, means tragedy) and so on are also network words willingly accepted by the public.

However, some network languages are too ridicule and entertaining. For example, homophonic characters are wrongly used to replace characters with the same sound by pinyin input method such as " 鸡冻 (ji dong) replacing 激动 (ji dong, means excitement)" , " 果酱 (guo jiang) replacing 过奖 (guo jiang, means overpraise)" , " 酱 紫 (jiang zi) replacing 这 样 子 (zhe yang zi, means like this)" , " 稀饭 (xi fan) replacing 喜欢 (xi huan), means (like)" , " 童鞋 (tong xie) replacing 同学 (tong xue, means classmate)" ; or numbers are used to replace original characters by spoonerism such as "748 (去死吧 qu si ba, means go to hell)" and "7456 (气死我了 qi si wo le, means I am so angry)" ;or acronyms of pinyin of Han characters are used to replace characters themselves such as "XDJM(兄弟姐妹 xiong di jie mei, means brothers and sisters)" , "MM(妹妹 mei mei, means younger sister)" and "BB(宝贝 bao bei, means baby)" ; or baby-talk is used such as " 东东 (dong dong)= 东西 (dong xi), means things)" , " 饭饭 (fan fan)= 吃饭 (chi fan, means to eat)" and " 片片 (pianpian)= 照片 (zhao pian, means photo)"; or English words and phrases and the spoonerism are used such as "OUT (出局 chu ju)" and "3Q (Thank you, 谢谢你 xie xie ni)" and so on. In fact, many of those words are wrong and whether they can be accepted by the public remains to be seen .

Some young people also self-create many four-character idioms like " 不明觉厉 (bu ming jue li)" , " 十动然拒 (shi dong ran ju)" and " 累觉不 爱 (lei jue bu ai)" , which make readers confused and don't know what is talking about. Young people like using characters like those and think they are concise and interesting. According to their explanations, " 不 明 觉 厉 (bu ming jue li)" refers to that although one does not know what he is talking about but still consider he is very shrewd; " 十动然拒 (shi dong ran ju)" refers to that one feels moved but still refuses and " 累觉不爱 (lei jue bu ai)" refers to that one is tired and feels that he will not have love again. It can be seen that such "network idioms" are the abbreviations of longer sentences. Although such game language is interesting in some way, it will give rise to communication barriers. We had better use the outstanding vocabularies handed down by Chinese nation.

In summary, many current network languages are inconsistent with the norms of Han characters, where Han characters tend to be used casually even vulgarly as a kind of symbols for recreation. If this trend continues, it will be a danger for Han characters. In August 2013, State Language Commission of the People's Republic of China issued General Standard Chinese Characters Table, which should be taken as criteria for learning and applying Han characters.

Appendix:
Chronological Table of the Chinese Dynasties

The Paleolithic Period	Approx. 1,700,000–10,000 years ago
The Neolithic Age	Approx. 10,000–4,000 years ago
Xia Dynasty	2070–1600 BC
Shang Dynasty	1600–1046 BC
Western Zhou Dynasty	1046–771 BC
Spring and Autumn Period	770–476 BC
Warring States Period	475–221 BC
Qin Dynasty	221–206 BC
Western Han Dynasty	206 BC–AD 25
Eastern Han Dynasty	25–220
Three Kingdoms	220–280
Western Jin Dynasty	265–317
Eastern Jin Dynasty	317–420
Northern and Southern Dynasties	420–589
Sui Dynasty	581–618
Tang Dynasty	618–907
Five Dynasties	907–960
Northern Song Dynasty	960–1127
Southern Song Dynasty	1127–1279
Yuan Dynasty	1206–1368
Ming Dynasty	1368–1644
Qing Dynasty	1616–1911
Republic of China	1912–1949
People's Republic of China	Founded in 1949